LOTUS 1-

2.4

Ernst Tiemeyer

LOTUS 1-2-3
2.4

PRISMA
COMPUTER
COURSE

Prisma Computer Courses first published in Great Britain 1992 by

McCarta Ltd
15 Highbury Place
London N5 1QP

Translation: George Hall
Production: LINE UP text productions

© Rowohlt Taschenbuch Verlag GmbH, Reinbek bei Hamburg
For the English translation
© 1992 Uitgeverij Het Spectrum BV, Utrecht

ISBN 1 85365 335 7

British Library Cataloguing-in-Publication Data.
A catalogue record for this book is available from the British Library.

Contents

Foreword

No other software package has achieved world-wide distribution to an extent comparable to Lotus 1-2-3. Throughout the entire world there are nine million users, making it, in fact, the industry standard. The numerous functions and the straightforward operation have resulted in this program constantly occupying a leading position according to sales and marketing statistics.

In Lotus 1-2-3, three essential elements of classical PC software have been combined: spreadsheets, charts and database management. Working with 'electronic worksheets', spreadsheets, is the central point in Lotus 1-2-3. Using these, it is possible to gather together all kinds of figures and calculations and to edit them. In order to present the numerical data in a clear and sophisticated manner, the integrated graphic module is one of the components of the package. In addition, it is possible to manage data files systematically and to use these in the processing.

In this book, we intend to illustrate the capabilities of the Lotus 1-2-3 integrated program. We shall deal with the current version 2.4 which is interesting for all users. A version 3.1 also exists, but to run this program an AT computer with a 80286 processor and 1 Mb internal memory are the minimum requirements. That version contains all the instructions and functions of the 2.4 version, plus a couple of extras. Accordingly, a beginner with version 3.1 can also make good progress using this book.

Using concrete examples, we shall outline the fundamental aspects of the instructions and functions of Lotus 1-2-3 in an explicit and systematic way, step by step. Important schemes are documented in checklists, allowing easy reference to problematic aspects, if any.

Of course, not all facets of the program can be described within the scope of this introduction. The inten-

tion is to give a systematic indication of the total operating area of Lotus 1-2-3. Foreknowledge is not essential. The book has been constructed in such a way that
the examples can be tried out immediately on the computer. In order to establish the new-found skills, exercises and solutions have been included at the end of
each chapter.

All the examples have been developed and tested on
an IBM compatible computer. The names of the keys
correspond to those on a standard IBM keyboard.

1   First steps with Lotus 1-2-3

Before being able to make optimal use of all the possibilities offered by Lotus, you must first become familiar with the fundamental concept of the program. This concerns knowledge of the application possibilities and the manner in which instructions are given.

1.1   Configuration conditions and areas of operation

Lotus 1-2-3 is an integrated program for the personal computer, providing a broad spectrum of possibilities. Spreadsheets are the focal point of the program. In order to use the program package, the following requirements must be fulfilled:

■ A personal computer (PC) with a minimum of 384 Kb internal memory (512 Kb if you want to use Wysiwig and the other add-ins that come with 1-2-3). The PC must have a harddisk and at least one floppy drive. The harddisk must have a minimum of approximately 2 Mb of available disk space.

■ The MS-DOS operating system, version 2.1 or more recent, which you will have received when purchasing the computer. The version of the operating system required depends on the type of computer.

Lotus 1-2-3 has three function areas which are operated identically:

■ **Spreadsheets**: the heart of the program. A spreadsheet is an electronic worksheet in which a large number of calculations can be made quickly. If there is any alteration in figures, the dependent results are recalculated.

■ **Charts**: recorded figures and data can be displayed

in orderly charts and diagrams for further processing or documentation. Available types are: line charts, bar charts in simple or stacked form, pie charts, XY charts and scatter charts.

■ **Databases**: using these, information can be stored in a structured way and selected or sorted in the light of certain criteria.

These three components are not separate from each other - exchange of data is possible. Information from a spreadsheet can be transferred to a database or vice versa and information from both modules can be presented in graphic form.

1.2 Installation

Installation of the program is necessary if you are going to work with Lotus 1-2-3 for the first time. During installation, the program will be adjusted to the demands of your hardware. The type of monitor, the diskdrives available, extended memory, graphic cards and output devices like printers and plotters are all taken into consideration.

In addition, it may be necessary to make use of the installation program later. This is the case, for example, if hardware components such as printers are replaced or added.

Before beginning the installation, have all the program diskettes ready in front of you.

Place the first diskette (Install) in drive A and proceed as follows:

■ Activate the installation program by typing:

```
A:INSTALL
```

■ Follow the instructions on the screen.

When the program has been started up, a screen show-
ing the following information will appear.

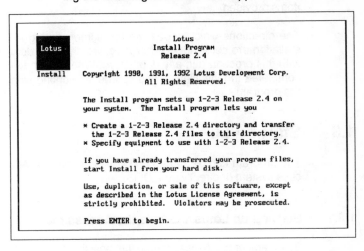

If you now press Enter, the main menu of the installation
program will appear:

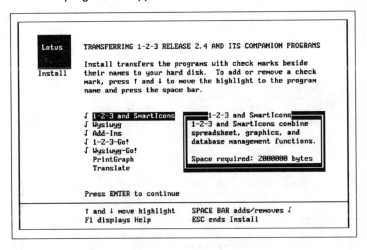

1-2-3 has a number of companion programs, which can
also be installed along with the 1-2-3 program itself. The

default setting is shown on the screen. If you wish to alter this, add or remove checkmarks in front of the items provided.

The directions which appear on the screen during installation are self-evident. Therefore, we shall not deal with this procedure in any depth here. When you have completed the installation, you can begin working with the program.

1.3   Starting up

The program can be started up by using either the Access system or directly from DOS.

1.3.1   Starting up Lotus 1-2-3 via the Access menu

By means of the Access menu, it is possible to make a choice from all the program elements. The menu is activated by typing the instruction:

```
lotus
```

On the screen which subsequently appears, you may choose one of the diverse possibilities.

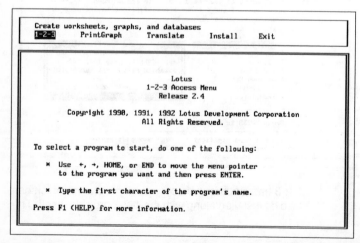

From the menu, select the name of the required program. Using the cursor keys to move left or right, go to the program and press Enter.

To activate the main program, select option 1-2-3. The other options have the following significance:

PrintGraph   Activates the program which prints the charts and diagrams which have been made using 1-2-3.

Translate   Utility program for exchanging data with other programs.

Install   Activates the installation program.

Exit   Ends working with Lotus 1-2-3.

Details about the use of these programs will be discussed more extensively later.

The advantage of the Access menu is that you can switch quickly and easily between 1-2-3 and the other programs. The highlight bar is normally located on the 1-2-3 option. You only need to move the bar using the cursor keys and to press Enter if you wish to select another program.

1.3.2   Starting up Lotus 1-2-3 directly from DOS

Activate the directory in which you have installed the program. Then type the command to activate the program:

123

This screen will appear:

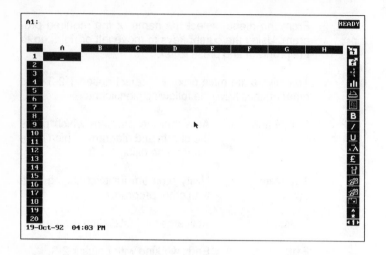

1.4   Operating principles

If you are going to work with Lotus 1-2-3 for the first
time, you will have to become familiar with the operating
principles. To do this, we shall examine the initial
screen a little more closely.

At the top of the opening screen, information is displayed concerning the status and the execution of the
instructions. The way in which the menu is activated is
important. This is done by pressing the slash (/). This
displays a list of the possible basic instructions, the
main menu, on the status line.

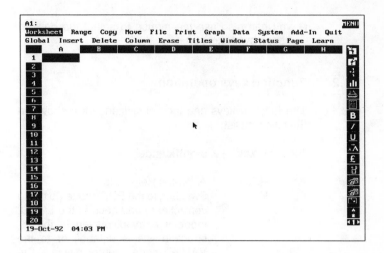

Lotus 1-2-3 is now ready to receive and implement commands. The basis for the execution of commands is formed by a combination of menu operation and operation of the function keys. Generally, a specified series of commands has to be activated. However, some commands should be, or must be, entered using the function keys F1 to F10.

Many functions can be activated by clicking on the icons at the right-hand side of the screen using the mouse. A brief description of the function in question is then given in the control panel. See also section 5.3.1 (Smart-Icons).

1.4.1 Menu operation

When you press the slash, a line containing the basic instructions appears at the top of the screen. Here you can make a choice, depending on the application. This can be done by:

- typing the first letter of the instruction or
- placing the cursor on the required instruction using the cursor keys and then pressing Enter or,

■ you can also use the mouse to select the desired
option by clicking on it.

1.4.2   Function keys operation

The function keys and their significance are shown in
the following list:

function key   significance

F1 HELP   Activates Help texts.

F2 EDIT   Switches to the EDIT mode (to make
               corrections) and back to the LABEL
               mode if entry displayed in the in-
               struction line is a label, or to the
               VALUE mode if entry displayed in
               the instruction line is a value.

F3 NAME   Displays a menu with range or file
               names.

F4 ABS   Converts a cell address to an abso-
               lute address or back to a relative ad-
               dress or mixed address.

F5 GOTO   Moves the cell pointer to a specified
               cell or range of cells.

F6 WINDOW   In the MENU mode, switches the
               display of dialogue boxes on and off.
               In the READY mode moves the cell
               pointer to the other window if the
               screen has been split.

F7 QUERY   In the READY mode, repeats the
               last /Data Query specified. In the
               FIND mode, switches 1-2-3 between
               the FIND mode and READY mode.

F8 TABLE   Repeats the most recent /Data
               Table operation.

F9 CALC   In the READY mode, recalculates all
               formulas in a worksheet. In the
               VALUE and EDIT modes, converts a
               formula to its current value.

F10 GRAPH   Draws the chart using the current
               parameters.

For beginners especially, and also in the case of spo-
radic usage, it is extremely helpful to make use of the
keyboard template supplied with the package. The significance of the function keys and the key combinations
are displayed on it. There are templates to fit the most
common keyboards.

1.4.3 Specifying and activating instructions

By activating an instruction, you can have the computer
execute required operations. The program has many instructions available, but using only a limited number of
these allows you to implement the basic steps in the
program.

If you wish to carry out a certain task using Lotus 1-2-3,
such as printing or saving a table, you should select the
appropriate instruction from the menu. We shall give an
example:

Imagine you wish to save a new table on a diskette.
First choose the File command by calling up the menu
by pressing the slash. Then press the letter F or use the
cursor keys to move to this option. In the subsequent
submenu, select the Save option. You can accept the
default value or adjust it to your own requirements.

The latter can be done by deleting the proposed file
name and directory or drive and then specifying your
own choice. Of course, it is quite reasonable to accept
the suggested name and drive. In that case, you simply
press Enter and the program implements the instruction. If there are no files as yet, no name will be shown
and you can enter a name yourself.

The following possibilities are available for specifying an
instruction in the case of a value proposed by the program:

■ confirm the suggestion of the program by pressing
   Enter

■ delete the default value using Esc and enter your own choice.

If, during the implementation of an instruction, you dis-cover that you have made a mistake, you can discon-tinue the entire procedure by pressing the Break key or by returning step by step to the main menu using the Esc key.

1.5   Using the Help function

Lotus 1-2-3 has a Help function which you can activate if you are no longer sure of what you must do to imple-ment an instruction. This function can be extremely handy especially in the initial stages.

The Help screen is activated by pressing F1, the Help key. You will then receive information concerning the topic activated by the choice of command.

Test the Help function by selecting the File Save in-struction. If you then press the F1 key, the following screen will appear:

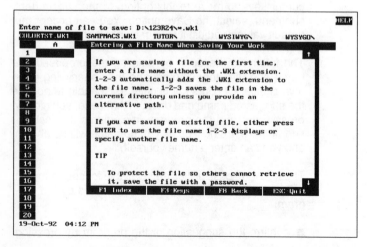

It is obvious that the information is relevant to the instruction you have just chosen. In addition, there is a menu at the bottom of the Help screen.

Help information can be summoned during any program activity, regardless of whether an instruction has been chosen or data is being entered. In addition, it is useful to request information if an error message appears while working with the program.

The Help function can be closed by pressing the Esc key. The program then returns to the screen from where you had activated the Help function.

1.6 Activating DOS instructions

From Lotus 1-2-3 it is possible to activate instructions from the operating system without having to exit the program completely. The System instruction enables you to do this.

Imagine you wish to use the DOS instruction DIR. Proceed as follows:

- Activate the instruction menu using the slash.
- Choose the System instruction by pressing S or by moving the cursor keys and pressing Enter.
- Type the DIR instruction on the DOS command line.
- Return to 1-2-3 using EXIT.

The last command returns you to the program. All DOS commands, excepting residential programs such as PRINT, may be used. These have to be activated before Lotus is started up (if the internal memory allows this). It is not possible to start up another program if you wish to return to 1-2-3.

1.7   Quitting the program

Lotus 1-2-3 is closed by using the Exit option. Before
quitting the program, it is advisable to save the file
which you have just been working on if you want to use
it again later. The program will ask you if you really want
to exit the program when you select the exit option.

Subsequently, the program will return to the Access
menu or the operating system, depending on the way in
which it has been started up. If the program has been
started up from DOS, the DOS prompt will reappear.

1.7.1   Summary of chapter 1

■ Lotus 1-2-3 is an integrated program for the personal
  computer, containing three function areas: spreadsheets, charts and diagrams and database management.
■ There are two possibilities to start up the 1-2-3 program: directly from the operating system or via the
  Access menu.
■ In addition to the actual 1-2-3 program there are separate programs for printing charts and diagrams, for
  installation and for the translation of files to comply
  with other programs.
■ Instructions in Lotus are generally given via menus.
  In addition, function keys are available for certain options. The mouse can also be used to select certain
  options by clicking directly on them.
■ The program possesses an integrated Help feature.
■ While working with Lotus 1-2-3, operating system instructions can be given by leaving the program temporarily via the System option in the main menu.

Exercises

(1)   Name the three function areas of Lotus 1-2-3.

(2)   Complete:

There are different ways of starting up Lotus 1-2-3. Using the _____ menu, all Lotus program elements can be selected from one menu. This menu contains, in addition to the actual program, the _____ option enabling you to print charts and diagrams and the _____ option for translating files from other programs.

(3)   Which keys should be used for:

(a) activating the instruction menu
(b) activating the Help feature
(c) quitting the Help screen?

Solutions

(1)   Spreadsheets, charts/diagrams and database management.

(2)   There are different ways of starting up Lotus 1-2-3. Using the *Access* menu all program elements can be selected from one menu. This menu contains, in addition to the actual program, the *PrintGraph* option enabling you to print charts and diagrams and the *Translate* option for translating files from other programs.

(3)   (a) /
       (b) F1
       (c) Esc.

2   Spreadsheets

2.1   Basic concept and application possibilities

Information which is processed in the office and in management in general, can frequently be represented in the form of tables. Making and editing tables using traditional methods is often rather laborious. This mostly involves considerable calculation and subsequent alteration leads to time-consuming recalculation.

Spreadsheets have been developed to deal with this kind of application. In this, an electronic form is created on the screen. The user is provided with a number of cells, a combination of rows and columns. These cells can be freely used. This electronic form is called a *spreadsheet* or *worksheet*.

In this worksheet, each cell consists of an empty space which can be filled in using text or numbers in the chosen application area. Formulas can also be entered, allowing relations between cells to be constructed. This provides the possibility of calculating several alternatives quickly and smoothly in the light of various data.

The following illustration shows a summary of the basic structure of a simple spreadsheet:

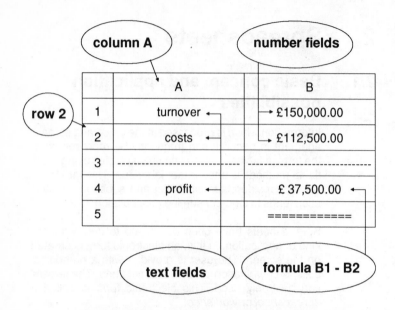

The application area of spreadsheet programs is extremely large. The main objective is the support of procedures concerning planning and management. Although applications dealing with company business management are clearly in the majority, there are also substantial possibilities within the technical and scientific fields and also, quite simply, in personal situations. The following summary shows examples of familiar applications within the three areas mentioned:

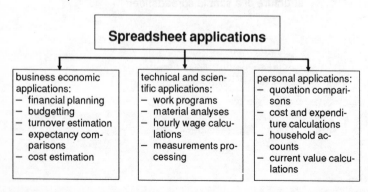

A spreadsheet can bring advantages even in the case of relatively small tables and, of course, the facility of operation and time-saving are greater the larger the tables and the more complex the formulas.

The most important benefits of a spreadsheet on the PC are:

Time-consuming and tedious calculation becomes unnecessary. This arises from the fact that the program can be used as a calculator. In addition, a large number of convenient functions are available, such as the determination of the sum or the calculation of the average value of a series of numbers, for which it is not necessary to introduce a difficult and lengthy formula.

Quick corrections (entering, deleting, superimposing) are simple to carry out. Later alterations to the form or contents, or correction of errors, are no exception when making monetary calculations. In cases like these, the computer program adjusts the form and the contents to the newly entered data. Often an immediate test is carried out on logical precision.

When number values are corrected, a recalculation of all relevant values takes place. Working with formulas makes a direct and rapid adjustment possible without extensive alterations to the spreadsheet.

Several versions of a problem solution can be worked out, for instance, various market or personnel situations.

Hypothetical questions can be easily solved. For example, using the returns figures per article, the change in the break-even point if the selling price of an article rises by a certain amount.

2.1.1   Summary of section 2.1

■ Spreadsheets provide an electronic form consisting of rows and columns.

■ Texts, numbers and formulas can be entered in the cells of the worksheet.

■ The application area of spreadsheet programs covers commercial, technical and personal requirements.

■ The most important benefits of spreadsheets are time-saving in the case of laborious calculation, easy correction and subsequent alteration, and projected calculation of alternatives.

2.2   The structure of the worksheet

The Lotus 1-2-3 program is able to make a table consisting of a maximum of 8192 rows and 256 columns. The points of intersection of the rows and columns are the *cells*. Thus, a table consists of a maximum of 2,097,152 cells (or fields) which can hold text, numbers or formulas.

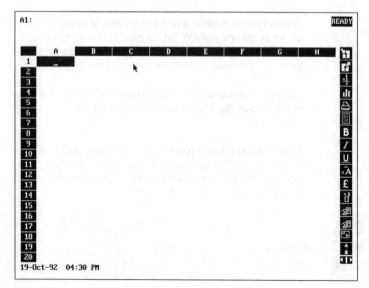

When Lotus 1-2-3 has been started up, the screen will
display a worksheet.(See page 28.)

The figure shows that only a small part of the total table
is visible. The cells contain no information as yet. The
assignment of contents to the cells occurs by entering
data or by calculation of formulas. In both cases, it is
necessary to determine the exact position of the cell by
specifying the appropriate column and row.

Each *column* is identified by one or two letters, the first
twenty-six with the letters A - Z, those following with AA
- ZZ, BA - BZ and so forth up to IV. The column indication is shown along the top of the worksheet.

Rows, on the other hand, are identified by numbers,
from 1 to 8192. The row numbers are located at the left-
hand side of the worksheet. In order to address a particular cell, it is necessary to specify a combination of
column letter and row number, such as A13 or B2.

The part of the table which is visible on the screen is
called the work area. Above this is the Control Panel. In
general, the work area contains an area of twenty rows
and eight columns which are nine characters wide. Accordingly, there are 160 cells of the table visible on the
screen. In one of these cells is the *cell pointer*, a small
bar inversely displayed. This indicates the current work
position and can be moved to another position on the
worksheet using the cursor keys or certain function
keys. The positioning of the cell pointer determines the
current cell to which the next entry or instruction will
apply.

The following summary indicates how the cell pointer
can be moved using the cursor or function keys:

position	**key(s)**
per column	cursor left/right
per row	cursor up/down
screen left/rightwards	Ctrl-cursor left/right

screen up/downwards	PgUp/PgDn
top left in spreadsheet	Home
jump in cursor direction	End, cursor key
lower right in active area	End, Home

As the cell pointer moves, the cell address changes. This is shown in the upper part of the screen, for example C6. The upper part first registers the information entered or displays the instructions which are to be activated if required. This is called the *Control Panel*. The main menu containing the commands can be activated by pressing the slash (/). This will produce a screen similar to that shown below.

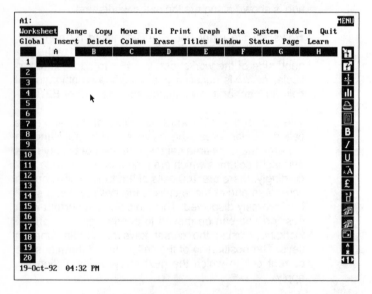

The figure shows that the upper part of the screen area consists of three lines.

■ On the first line, various information about the current cell is displayed. If the cell contains any data, it will also be shown here. In addition, if applicable, the column width, the format and the protection status will be displayed. We shall return to this later. At the far right, the current status of the worksheet is shown, for example MENU. This indicates the conditions under which work is taking place at the moment: READY, LABEL, MENU etc.

■ The main or submenu is shown on the second line. In the READY mode which can be activated using Esc, the information which has been entered is shown before it is placed in the current cell. Just to try this out, press the Esc key and enter the word 'test'. Then activate the MENU mode once more by pressing Esc again and then the slash.

■ The third line displays a further description of the command which is highlighted in the main or submenu. In some cases a request for data entry may also be shown here.

The current date and time are displayed in the lower left-hand corner. Using the Worksheet Global Default Other option, this display can be switched off or given another format.

2.2.1 Summary of section 2.2

■ Lotus 1-2-3 provides an electronic worksheet consisting of 8192 rows and 256 columns. The combination of rows and columns produces cells in which data are entered.

■ Columns are indicated by letters, rows by numbers.

■ When addressing a cell, the column is specified first, then the row.

■ The Lotus 1-2-3 screen has two main areas: the Control Panel at the top and the work area which normally consists of 160 cells.

2.3   Preparing a table

That there are many applications for the spreadsheet has already been mentioned. However, before you begin to solve a practical problem using the computer, it is useful to thoroughly analyse the nature of the problem. Only then will you be sure that a spreadsheet will be created which provides the desired solution. The greater the consideration, the smaller the chance of errors.

In order to make a efficient calculation model, the following questions should be answered:

■ Which kind of results should the computer come up with?
■ Which information is needed to solve the problem?
■ Which calculations need to be carried out to produce the desired results?

2.3.1   Altering the default settings

Lotus 1-2-3 has default settings for a number of things, including the width of the individual columns and the way in which texts are aligned. General planning may make it useful to change some of these settings.

The standard width for columns is nine characters, texts which are entered are left-aligned and numbers are shown as real numbers. These default settings can be altered using the Worksheet Global submenu which appears as follows:

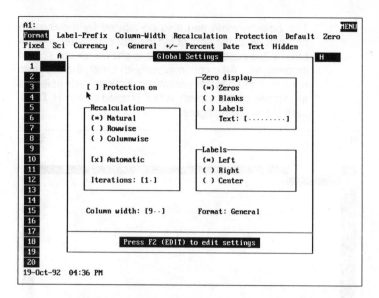

These commands also make it possible to specify the
type of recalculation, protection throughout the entire
worksheet and the definition of certain parameters
when creating worksheets. Here, you can think of the
unit of currency, the date and time format and the type
of printer.

2.3.2 Changing the default column width

In the following example, we shall determine the column
width as being twelve characters. Proceed as follows:

- Press the slash to activate the menu.
- Select Worksheet (press Enter), Global (Enter) using
  the cursor keys or by pressing W and G.
- Select Column-Width using the cursor keys (and
  Enter) or by pressing C
- Specify the desired column width 12.
- Confirm the command using Enter.

The column width can also be altered by moving the
cursor keys to the right or left instead of entering a number. In this case, the alteration is shown on the screen
immediately. After confirmation with Enter, the program
returns to the original worksheet. Now only six columns
are visible on the screen, A to F instead of A to H. Compare the following figure:

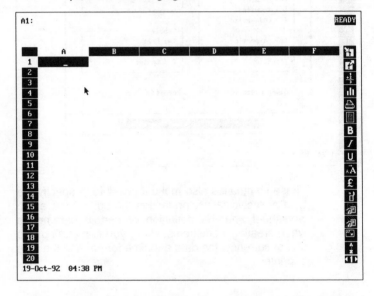

The column width 12 is now standard for all columns in
the worksheet. Nevertheless, it remains possible to allocate a certain width to individual columns. The command Worksheet Column enables you to alter the width
for particular columns, while the other columns retain
the standard width. Columns may have a width of 1 to
240 characters.

2.3.3   Altering the default alignment

The alignment of text also has a standard setting. In
general, texts (labels) are left-aligned throughout the
whole worksheet. Changes to this can be made using

the command Worksheet Global Label-Prefix. Other options consist of Right and Center. In order to make Right
the standard setting, proceed as follows:

■ Go to the command menu using the slash.
■ Select the option Worksheet Global using W and G or
  the cursor keys.
■ Select the Label-Prefix option from the submenu
  using L or the cursor keys.
■ Select the Right option by pressing R or by using the
  cursor keys and press Enter.

In order to prevent misunderstandings in the rest of this
book, it is advisable to repeat this exercise once more,
but now choose Left instead of Right. Labels in the
worksheet will be standard left-aligned again.

2.3.4   Altering the default number format

In Lotus 1-2-3, numbers are normally displayed as real
numbers. This applies both to numbers which are entered and to results which are calculated. In this, the
values are registered to a precision of fifteen decimal
points regardless of the format used.

The default setting of numeric values can be altered
using the command Worksheet Global Format. In the
submenu which is subsequently shown, the following
options are available:

Fixed	for display of fixed number of decimals
Sci	scientific, for display in exponential form
Currency	for display of numbers with a particular unit of currency
, (comma)	for separation of thousands
General	standard display in real numbers
+/-	for display as bar chart
Percent	to add the percentage symbol
Date	to choose a certain notation for date and time (five date and four time methods of no-tation are possible)

Text   to display formulas on the screen
Hidden   to suppress display of information on the
            screen.

Note: It is possible to view the current global settings or
other settings by using the Worksheet Status instruction. The following will appear on the screen:

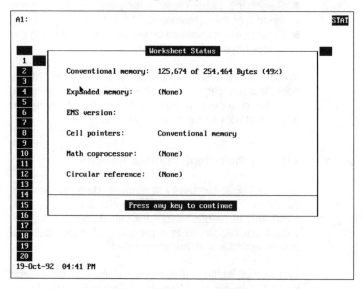

On this screen, detailed information concerning memory used, the global parameters and certain hardware
options is shown. You return to the worksheet by pressing a random key.

2.3.5   Determining the calculation method

The order of sequence of calculation is standard in as
much as the value of a formula is calculated only when
all the values needed to make the calculation are
known. This default setting can be changed using the
Worksheet Global Recalculation command. Available
options are:

- Natural: the value of a formula is calculated only when all the values needed to make the calculation are known.
- Columnwise: the values for column A are calculated first, then for column B etc.
- Rowwise: the values for row 1 are calculated first, then for row 2 etc.
- Automatic: when the contents of a cell have been altered, the worksheet is immediately recalculated.
- Manual: when the contents of a cell have been altered, the table is recalculated only after the CALC key (F9) has been pressed.
- Iteration: enables repeated calculation.

2.3.6 Protecting worksheet cells

In many instances, especially in the case of formula fields, it is advisable to make alteration to cells impossible. Using the Worksheet Global Protection command, you are able to determine whether the protection of the cells should be active or not. In this way, you can prevent information in cells being overwritten unintentionally. The precondition here is that the global protection is switched on and the cell is protected.

The cell protection can also be selective, i.e. applicable to parts of a table. Use the command Worksheet Range Prot to do this and Worksheet Range Unprot if you wish to discontinue the protection.

2.3.7 Setting default values for the program start

Lotus 1-2-3 has various options in the submenu Worksheet Global Default. Here, it is possible to specify certain parameters which are valid from the start of the program.

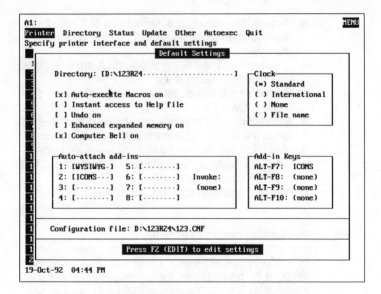

This concerns, among others:

- the type of printer and the printer port (Printer option)
- the directory for activating files (Directory option)
- the display of current parameters (Status option)
- diverse international display formats (Others option).

The Others option also enables you to automatically load an add-in at the start of 1-2-3.

2.3.8   Summary of section 2.3

- Before deciding to assign a problem to the computer, you should first consider the structure and the format of the worksheet.
- The default setting for column width can be altered using the Worksheet Global Column-Width instruction.
- The default setting for the alignment of texts (labels) can be altered using the Worksheet Global Label-Prefix instruction.

■ The default setting for the display of numbers can be altered using the Worksheet Global Format instruction.

2.4 Making a Lotus table: entering cell data

When all settings have been defined, the input of data can begin. This takes place using the keyboard. A clear distinction must be made between the following forms:

■ input of text called 'labels' in Lotus
■ input of numbers
■ input of formulas for calculation.

It is advisable to first enter the texts and the independent number values and then the formulas which make it possible to interconnect cells.

In order to learn the basis functions of the Lotus spreadsheet, we shall get down to work with the exercise 'Turnover calculation'.

Exercise 2-1: Turnover calculation

Create a Lotus table to solve the following problem:

Based on the estimated monthly turnover, the expected annual turnover and the maximum and minimum monthly turnover are to be calculated. The result should be displayed in the following form:

	Turnover x
Month	**£1000**
January	150
February	212
March	222
April	318
May	344
June	551
July	180
August	166
September	300
October	345
November	433
December	335
Total	3556
Maximum	551
Minimum	150

2.4.1   Entering text

A fundamental rule when making any entry at all is that
you first have to go to the cell where the input is to be
made. In the example shown, we should select A2 as
the active cell.

When text is being entered, it appears initially in the top
part of the screen. Simultaneously, the mode block in
the top right-hand corner changes from READY to
LABEL. For this reason, text input is often referred to as
label input. When you have entered the word 'Month',
the screen will appear as follows:

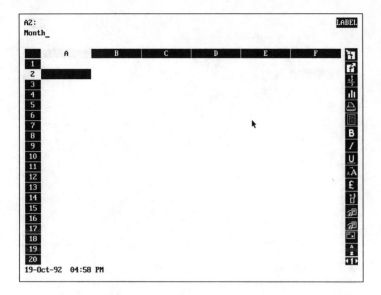

As mentioned, the characters entered do not appear directly in the table, but on a line in the upper part of the screen, under the indication of the cell position. In order to move the text to the cell, you have to press Enter. The text is then moved to the active cell in the table and the mode changes again from LABEL to READY. Compare the following figure:

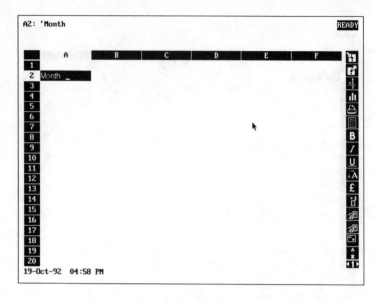

As well as using the Enter key, text can also be moved to the cell by means of one of the cursor keys. This can be useful if a series of texts has to be entered, since the following cell is immediately activated for the registration of new text. If you press a cursor key, the cell pointer is moved in the worksheet in accordance with the direction of the cursor key and the next input can take place.

The general procedure for the input of a series of texts is as follows:

- Place the cell pointer at the first input cell.
- Enter the text.
- Confirm the input using Enter or activate the next cell using one of the cursor keys.
- Enter the next text.
- Confirm the input using Enter or one of the cursor keys.

Normally, the texts which have been entered are left-aligned in the current cell of the table.

This is clear in the figure below:

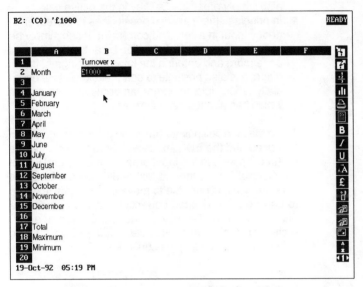

(Note that you have to type a ' before entering the pound sign, otherwise the program will read this as a number instead of as a text.)

In addition, you will observe that if information has already been entered in a cell, it will be removed if new information is entered there. The previous information is then irretrievably lost.

Nevertheless, it will undoubtedly occur that when entering information you will place it in the wrong cell or you may forget a character. In cases like these, the following correction possibilities are available:

■ If an error is seen directly at the input, it can be corrected using the Backspace key.
■ Using Esc, a text which has been typed but not yet transported to the cell can be cancelled.
■ If you have accidentally placed information in a cell where no information should be located, you can

undo this using the /Range Erase command. You can also simply press the Del key in the active cell.

■ In principle, there are two possibilities to correct erroneous input in a cell. The correct input can simply be written over the old information by activating the cell once more and entering the information again. In addition, it is also possible to edit the text. This is especially applicable to larger amounts of information which has already been entered.

To do this, the cell pointer has to be placed on the cell to be edited and the EDIT mode activated by pressing the F2 function key. In the input area, on the second line of the Control Panel, the old text is displayed. Using the cursor keys, it is possible to move through this text and to carry out the desired corrections at the appropriate places, using the Del key if required. Confirm the corrections using Enter (in this case, it is not possible to confirm the input using the cursor keys).

2.4.2   Entering numbers

When the text data have been entered, you can continue with the number values which are already known. Activate the cell in which the input should be placed, B4 for instance. In the case of a number, the program registers that immediately. The mode block changes directly from READY to VALUE, while the number remains in the input area. After confirmation using Enter, the number is adopted by the activated cell and the mode changes again to READY.

The general procedure when entering values is as follows:

■ Activate the cell which is to receive information using the cursor keys.
■ Enter the value.
■ Confirm the input using Enter or one of the cursor keys.

The Enter key is normally used if you do not have to enter any more numbers. If numbers have to be entered consecutively, it is better to make use of the cursor keys to directly activate the next cell. Now enter all the numbers from the example. Correction of numbers input takes place in the same way as with text input. When all information has been entered, the table should appear as in the table below:

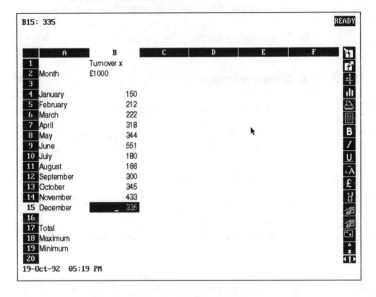

There is one thing which is immediately obvious - in contrast to the text, the numbers are right-aligned.

Note:

■ In Lotus 1-2-3, information can be entered in various formats. For example, a number can be entered as a percentage (e.g. 50%) or as an exponential value (5.23E+0.3). We shall return to this topic later.

■ A number must begin with a cypher or with one of the following characters: . + - (£. You can change the currency sign that Lotus 1-2-3 accepts as initial character of a number using the Default International Settings screen (Worksheet Global Default Other International).

■ A number can consist of a maximum of 240 characters.

■ Spaces and commas are not valid when entering thousands. In addition only one decimal point may be specified in a number.

■ If the number entered is broader than the column, a series of asterisks is shown in this cell. However, this does not influence the number stored in memory. If the column is widened, the number is displayed in full.

■ The decimal separator is the point.

2.4.3   Entering formulas

Using formulas, a relation can be created between two or more cells in a table, and thus results can be calculated automatically. In addition, it is possible to quickly work out the variants arising from a certain problem.

The general components of a formula are:

■ independent values, for example 14, -5
■ cell addresses, for example A13
■ certain calculation signs, the so-called *operators*.

In complex applications, a formula may also consist of strings (texts, like names), range specifications (see section 2.10) and functions (the so-called @-functions).

Formula structure

In the case of formula input, it is necessary to first activate the cell in which the required result is to be placed. Subsequently, you should specify, by entering a plus (+), that a formula is about to be entered. Then the formula may be entered.

Procedure for formulas in 1-2-3:

■ No spaces may occur in formulas, except within text in text formulas.
■ A formula may consist of a maximum of 240 charac-ters.
■ A plus sign must precede a formula if a cell address is specified instead of a number.
■ Knowledge of the calculation signs is essential for the formal structure of the formula.

The calculation signs, which activate the execution of certain operations, are also called *operators*. The im-portant operators in Lotus 1-2-3 are listed below:

operator	significance	rank
^	power	7 (highest)
+	positive value	6
-	negative value	6
*	multiply	5
/	divide	5
+	add	4
-	subtract	4
=	equals	3
<	smaller than	3
<=	smaller than or equal to	3
>	greater than	3
>=	greater than or equal to	3
<>	not equal to	3
#NOT#	logical negative	2
#AND#	logical AND relation	1
#OR#	logical OR relation	1
&	string link	1 (lowest)

In the summary, in addition to the significance of the various operators, a hierarchical rank number has been allocated. This indicates the order in which Lotus 1-2-3 executes the calculations if several operators are in-cluded in the formula. The rules applying to this are:

■ Operations with a high rank number are implemented first.
■ In the case of operations with the same rank number, the calculation takes place from left to right.
■ If brackets are included, the operations between the brackets are executed first. Within the brackets the rank numbers remain valid.

Examine the following formula. The order of execution is shown underneath:

```
A13-A5((A7+20)*0.13)/450
  4      1    2      3
```

In the example dealing with the calculation of turnover, formulas have to be entered in cells B17, B18 and B19. We shall first deal with the formula in B17. This allows us to acquaint ourselves with the structure and the fundamental procedure of working with formulas.

There are various methods of entering a formula in a table in Lotus 1-2-3:

(a)   Constructing a formula by specifying the cell positions

You enter the formula by specifying the cell positions which are necessary for the calculation. These are linked to each other using the required operators. In order to calculate the sum of the turnovers for field B17, you must enter the following:

```
+B4+B5+B6+B7+B8+B9+B10+B11+B12+B13+B14+B15
```

When the formula has been placed in the input area, the following will be shown on the screen:

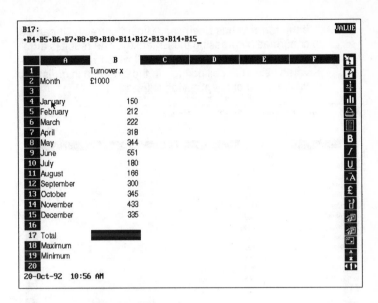

Confirmation of the input using Enter places the correct result in cell B17.

(b) Constructing a formula by positioning the cell pointer

Positioning the cell pointer is a quicker method of specifying the cells which are necessary for the calculation. After activating the result field and pressing the plus key (+), the cell pointer can be moved over the cells which form part of the calculation. When an operator has been specified or the Enter key has been pressed, the pointer will return to the result cell. In this way, a formula will be constructed identical to the one above.

(c) Constructing a formula using names for cell identification

This procedure facilitates addressing individual cells when working with individual cells and cell ranges in larger tables. We shall deal with this extensively later.

If the formula has been constructed correctly, it can be confirmed by pressing the Enter key. The result is automatically placed in the result cell which has been activated using the cell pointer. In the example in question, this result should appear as follows:

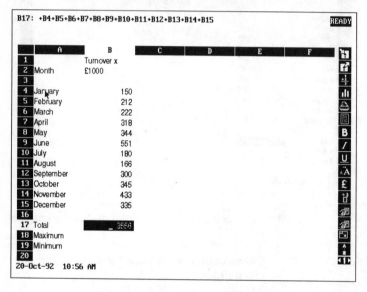

The diagram shows the result in cell B17: 3556. At the same time, the corresponding formula is displayed on the top line of the screen. Formulas which are not formally correct are not accepted by Lotus 1-2-3. This is recognizable by the acoustic signal (peep) emitted by the computer. A common error, for example, is the entry of a space before or after an operator. In a case like this, the formula entered can be changed in the EDIT mode (F2 key) just like an erroneous result.

Different types of formulas can be constructed in Lotus 1-2-3. In our example, we have used an *arithmetic formula* to calculate the sum. The calculations take place using number values (numeric data) and mathematical operators.

Another type of formula is the text formula. In this, the texts (labels) are linked using the string operator (&). Finally, there are the logical formulas. Here, values which occur in two or more cells are compared to each other using the comparison operators AND, OR, and NOT, and the result is placed in an apart cell. We shall return to this topic later.

The following checklist gives a summary of the procedures using arithmetical formulas:

■ Activate the result cell using the cursor keys.
■ Select the correct mode for entering formulas by pressing the plus sign.
■ Enter the formula, for example B4+B5+...
■ Confirm the input using Enter.

In order to display a cell formula later, you only have to place the cell pointer in that cell. The corresponding formula will then be shown on the first line of the Control Panel.

Constructing formulas using functions

The formulas which Lotus 1-2-3 provides can save the user a great deal of work. Among other things, there are functions for calculating the sum and for the determination of maximum and minimum values.

The general formulation of the sum function is as follows:

```
@SUM (list)
```

Using this function, you can calculate the sum of a row or column, and also the sum of numbers in random cells. In our example, you should proceed as follows:

■ Activate the result cell B17 using the cursor keys.
■ Activate the function by typing the at sign (@).
■ Enter the function name: SUM.

■ Place the arguments behind it between brackets, as
follows: (B4..B15).
■ Confirm the input using Enter.

If you have done everything properly, the screen should
look like this:

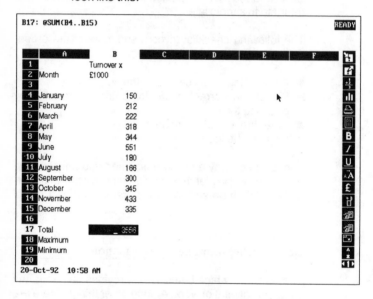

When using the mouse, you can also use the third icon
from the top for addition formulas.

All functions begin with an at sign. Then a key word
must be specified, SUM in our example. Subsequently,
the corresponding cell range should be placed between
brackets. When determining the cell range, the following rules are applicable:

■ First specify the position of an outer (corner) cell.
■ Then type two points (the range operator).
■ Finally specify the other outermost cell.

It is also possible to specify an outer cell by moving to it
using the cursor keys.

In this way, the maximum and minimum values can be calculated using the appropriate functions: the maximum value using @MAX(list) and the minimum value using @MIN(list).

In all cases, the rule is that in the result cell first the corresponding function name, preceded by the at sign, and then the range or the values for the calculation should be entered between brackets. If several arguments occur between the brackets, they should be separated by a semi-colon. For example:

```
@SUM(B4..B6;B9..B12)
```

In order to carry out our example, the exercise 'Turnover calculation', we require the following formulas:

```
B17 = @SUM(B4..B15)
B18 = @MAX(B4..B15)
B19 = @MIN(B4..B15)
```

When all commands have been confirmed using the Enter key, the following table is the result:

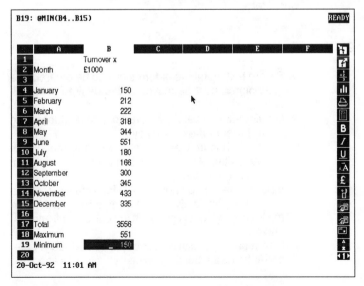

You have now become acquainted with the first group of functions which Lotus 1-2-3 provides - the statistical functions, also called the arithmetical functions. Other functions of this type are:

- average: @AVG(list)
- standard deviation: @STD(list)
- variance: @VAR(list)
- count entries: @COUNT(list).

In addition to statistical functions, Lotus 1-2-3 also provides the following other types of functions:

- mathematical functions
- logical functions
- financial functions
- date and time functions
- string functions
- database statistical functions
- special functions.
- Add-In functions

Examples of the most important functions will be dealt with later.

2.4.4   Summary of section 2.4

- Before text, numbers or formulas can be entered, the cell pointer must be moved to the desired cell position.
- Confirmation of values entered can take place using either Enter or the cursor keys.
- Input which is neither a number nor a formula is regarded as text (label). A cell can contain a maximum of 240 characters.
- Input is checked by Lotus 1-2-3 for formal errors. An acoustic signal is given if an error is registered. Formally correct input is stored in the current cell and displayed.
- Erroneous input can be corrected immediately. Later correction can best be executed by activating the

EDIT mode (F2 key) or by overwriting the old information with the new.

■ The following information can be placed in a formula: number values, strings, cell addresses, range names and @ functions. They are linked using operators.

■ The use of functions considerably simplifies the input of formulas.

2.5 Working with files

You have now made the first table in Lotus 1-2-3. Normally, you would intend to use this table again at a later date. Thus, the table should be saved on disk. The commands which have a bearing on working with files are located in the File command in the main menu. Select this option using /F and the following screen will appear:

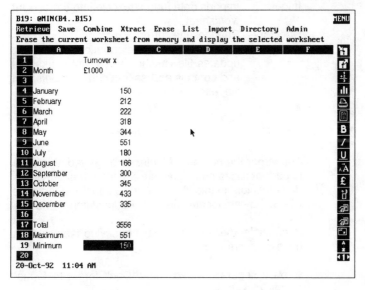

The options in this submenu have the following significance:

option   significance

Retrieve   Activates a file which can be edited. You
            can also click on the second icon from the
            top of the icon palette.

Save   Saves a created file. You can also click on
            the first icon from the top of the icon palette.

Combine   Combines different files. This can transport
            parts of a saved file to the current work-
            sheet.

Xtract   Saves part of the current worksheet. Ac-
            cordingly, with a selection of information
            you are able to make a smaller worksheet
            from a larger one.

Erase   Deletes a file on disk.

List   Displays a list of files in the current direc-
            tory.

Import   Imports data from a text file into the current
            worksheet.

Directory   Changes the current directory.

Admin   Creates a table of information about files,
            updates file links in the current worksheet
            and controls access to a current worksheet
            file reservation.

2.5.1   Specifying drive and directory

The larger the number of tables to be edited, the more
important it is to organize the file management in an orderly fashion. In this, the file names and the directories
where they are located are of the utmost importance.

In principle, there are two ways of saving tables which
have been created:

■ on a separate workdiskette. Don't forget to format
new diskettes.

■ on the harddisk, if available. Make regular backups to
safeguard your information.

It is sometimes necessary to change directory or drive.

This takes place in Lotus 1-2-3 using the File Directory command.

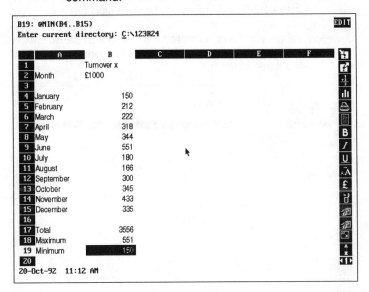

```
B19: @MIN(B4..B15)                                          EDIT
Enter current directory: C:\123R24
```

	A	B	C	D	E	F
1		Turnover x				
2	Month	£1000				
3						
4	January	150				
5	February	212				
6	March	222				
7	April	318				
8	May	344				
9	June	551				
10	July	180				
11	August	166				
12	September	300				
13	October	345				
14	November	433				
15	December	335				
16						
17	Total	3556				
18	Maximum	551				
19	Minimum	150				
20						

```
20-Oct-92  11:12 AM
```

The current directory is shown first, for example C:\123R24. You can specify another directory (and drive) here. After pressing Enter to confirm, the program will return to the READY mode. If you wish to change the current directory in drive A, proceed as follows:

■ Select the File Directory submenu using /FD.
■ Type 'a:'.
■ Confirm the new choice using Enter.

If required, you may add an existing path name to the input at the second stage.

2.5.2 Saving a file

As soon as you know where a file is to be stored, you can activate the command which actually saves the file. Using the File Save command, you can save a file on

disk which you have just created or edited. We shall
now save our example file under the name TURNOVR1
in the 123R24 directory on the harddisk C.

When you have activated the submenu, the following
screen will appear in which you are requested to specify
the name of the file:

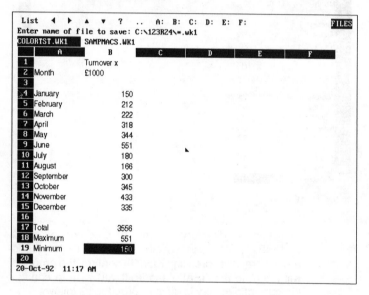

Firstly, the default name C:\123R24*.WK1 appears, in
which the different components have the following significance:

■ C:\ stands for the drive which is specified in the standard settings and which is registered in the configuration file.
■ The current directory is indicated behind the backslash.
■ *.WK1 indicates that a worksheet file with the extension .WK1 will be created.

When specifying file names the following rules apply:

- there is a maximum of eight characters, followed by a period and three letters for the extension if necessary
- capital letters, small letters, numbers and underline characters are all allowed
- no spaces
- no special characters.

If you specify a name which already exists, you must confirm that the former file should be replaced by the new one. Otherwise, choose Cancel or press the Esc key which discontinues the command and the old file is retained. In addition, it is possible to make a backup copy. The former file receives the extension .BAK and the new version is saved under the existing name.

In the example, we are dealing with a file which is to be saved for the first time. We shall give it the name TURNOVR1. Proceed as follows:

- Select the File Save submenu using /FS.
- Specify the name 'turnovr1'.
- Confirm this using Enter.

When the confirmation has been given, the file is saved in the current directory. Both the worksheet data and the specified parameters (format, print options) are saved.

As you will observe, it is not difficult to save a file. Nevertheless, it is important to keep the following points in mind:

- The file can be saved in a particular directory by explicitly specifying a drive and directory in front of the file name.
- When saving, Lotus 1-2-3 automatically assigns an extension which indicates which type of file it is. In the case of worksheet files that is .WK1, with graphic files that is .PIC and with print files that is .PRN.
- If the worksheet file is too large for the chosen disk, an error message will appear on the screen. Discontinue the saving process by pressing the Esc key and

make space available or choose another disk. Then
repeat the process to save the file.

■ If the saving process is repeated, the previous file
name is allocated as default name. Confirm this using
Enter or assign a new name by cancelling the default
name by pressing Esc twice and then enter the new
name, for example 'turnovr2'. Then there will be two
files, TURNOVR1.WK1 and TURNOVR2.WK1.

As an extra service, Lotus 1-2-3 provides the possibility
of entering a password along with the file when saving
it. In this way, you can prevent non-authorized persons
activating the file. The file can then only be activated if
the password is given. Proceed as follows:

■ Activate the File Save submenu using /FS.
■ Press Esc twice and enter a new name, but do not
press Enter yet.
■ Enter a space behind the file name and add the letter
P. Now press Enter.
■ The program requests a password. Specify a word of
not more than 15 letters.
■ Confirm using Enter.
■ The program asks for confirmation. Specify the same
word once more.
■ Confirm the input using Enter.

The password may consist of a maximum of fifteen letters. Spaces are not allowed. The characters are not
visible on the screen during input - a small block appears instead. The password should be repeated to
avoid the wrong word being recorded unintentionally.
This could lead to problems later when loading the file.

A password can always be subsequently removed or altered. To do this, the file must first be loaded and then
the File Save command activated. Specify the name,
press the spacebar and activate the password option
using P. Remove the previous password using the Esc
key and you can now assign a new word. You may also
remove the previous password without replacing it. In
that case, remove the previous password using the

Backspace key and then press Enter. Of course, it is important to remember a password or to keep it in a safe place. A protected file cannot be loaded without the correct password.

Saving only a part instead of the entire worksheet is also a possibility. In this case, select the File Xtract option. You can then save, for example, only the formulas or values if you wish.

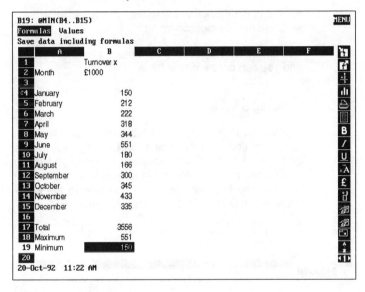

The diagram shows that there are two options:

■ **Formulas**: only the formulas in the current worksheet are saved in the file extract.
■ **Values**: numbers and texts and results are saved in a separate extract, but no formulas.

The general procedure is as follows:

■ Activate the File Xtract submenu using /FX.
■ Select the required option: Formulas or Values.
■ Specify a file name for the extract file.

■ Specify the range which is to be saved.
■ Confirm using Enter.

Caution: Do not use this command to save information with the intention of using it in another
program.

If you wish to create another table, you must select the
Worksheet Erase option. Proceed as follows:

■ Select the Worksheet Erase submenu using /WE.
■ Confirm the selection using Y.

The current worksheet will be removed from the screen
and you can create a new table.

2.5.3   Loading a table

If you wish to edit or print a table which you have already created, you must first load the table from the
disk. The File Retrieve command enables you to do
this. Before loading a file, remember to save the current
file first. The File Retrieve command deletes the worksheet which is in memory at that moment.

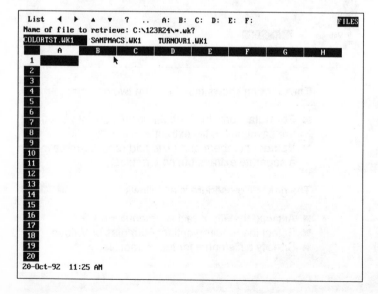

The figure shows that Lotus 1-2-3 lists the file names. The file list is shown as soon as the File Retrieve command is activated. If present, subdirectories are also displayed. On the second line, you will see a request to specify the name of the file to be loaded. The default name is C:\123R24*.WK? which means:

- that drive C is current
- that directory 123R24 is current
- that a file with the extension .WK1 or .WKS can be loaded.

The marking bar is located on the line below on the first name in the list. In our case, that is COLORTST.WK1. If you wish to load this file, proceed as follows:

- Select the File Retrieve submenu using /FR.
- Press Enter to confirm the default name COLORTST.WK1.

The chosen table will subsequently appear on the screen.

When selecting a file to load there are two possibilities:

- You can specify a file name yourself. In this, the name must be identical to the name saved with the file.
- Select a file from the list.

With the second option, having activated the File Retrieve submenu, you can move through the file names using the cursor keys. The names are arranged in alphabetical order. When you have selected a file using the cursor keys, confirm this choice using Enter and the table will appear on the screen. At first, there is only one line with file names visible. If you wish to have a complete list of files and directories displayed, you can activate the total list using the NAME key, F3. This can produce the following screen, for instance:

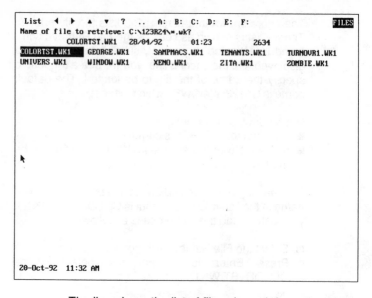

The line above the list of files shows information about the file which is highlighted at that moment, such as the date of last edition and the size. Pressing F3 once more will return you to the File menu.

It is also possible to load a file directly without it being in the current directory. To do this, you must specify the path which leads to the file in front of the file name. For example, to open the file FIRM92 in the directory EXPEND, you should specify:

```
\EXPEND\FIRM92
```

Files which are protected by a password receive special treatment. If you load a file which has been protected with a password, you will observe that you must first give the password in order to load this protected file.

A file which is located in the current directory can also be automatically loaded at the start of the program. A precondition is that the file must be saved under the name AUTO123. This worksheet is then displayed on the screen each time Lotus 1-2-3 is started up.

2.5.4 Displaying existing file names

When saving and loading files, after the corresponding command has been activated, the names of the files are displayed on one line on the Control Panel. When a file name has been specified, the list disappears from the screen.

The display of file names can be extended by pressing the function key F3, the NAME key. The list of files present is displayed over the entire screen. The cursor keys can be used to make a choice.

The extended display can also be activated using the File List command. This can be useful, for instance, to check which files are still in a directory after a deletion process. To do this, proceed as follows:

■ Select the File List submenu using /FL.
■ Select the desired option.

The result of this is that the worksheet is temporarily replaced by a summary of all files of the chosen type in the current directory. The following options are available:

■ Worksheet (files with the extension .WK1).
■ Print (files with the extension .PRN).
■ Graph (files with the extension .PIC).
■ Other (all files in the current directory).
■ Link (all files on disk which are linked to the current worksheet).

If there are no files in the current directory with the corresponding extension, the program will return to the READY mode.

2.5.5 Deleting a stored file

Files on disk which are no longer in use can be deleted using the File Erase command. When you have acti-

vated the submenu, options appear enabling you to select the type of file you wish to erase: Worksheet, Print,
Graph, Other. These options have the following significance when dealing with the current directory:

■ Worksheet: all files with the extensions .WK1 and
  .WKS are displayed.
■ Print: all files with the extension .PRN (for printer) are
  displayed.
■ Graph: all files with the extension .PIC are displayed.
■ Other: all files are displayed.

A file which has been deleted using these commands
cannot be recalled, not even with the UNDO command
(Alt-F4). The information in that file is irretrievably lost in
principle, although utility programs may be able to help
you to some extent.

When you have made a choice, the names of all files
which can be deleted will be shown. Using the cursor
keys, move to the file you wish to delete and confirm
your choice using Enter. The file will only be deleted
when you again confirm the deletion with Yes. In order
to delete the file GEORGE, proceed as follows:

■ Select the submenu File Erase using /FE.
■ Select the Worksheet option by pressing Enter.
■ Move to the GEORGE file using the cursor keys.
■ Press Enter and confirm by pressing Enter once
  again.

Here, you may also directly select a file which is not in
the current directory. To do this, you must specify the
appropriate path when entering the file name.

2.5.6   Summary of section 2.5

■ A file is saved on disk using the command File Save.
  You must then specify the name of the file. The file
  may be protected by a password if desired.
■ An existing worksheet can be edited via the File Re-

trieve submenu. It is then shown on the screen.
- Using the File List command, a list of files which are located in the current or specified directory can be displayed.
- Files are deleted from disk via the File Erase submenu.

2.6 Extending a table by copying

We shall now extend the table TURNOVR1.WK1. Here, the command COPY can be extremely useful in saving a great deal of input work. The following example will make this clear:

Exercise 2-2: Extending a table by copying

Next to the column in the original table, another column must be created in which the percentage of the turnover per month should be registered. The result of the new table should appear as shown:

Month	Turnover x £1000	Share in %
january	150	4.2
february	212	6.0
march	222	6.2
april	318	8.9
may	344	9.7
june	551	15.5
july	180	5.1
august	166	4.7
september	300	8.4
october	345	9.7
november	433	12.2
december	335	9.4
total	3556	
maximum	551	
minimum	150	

2.6.1   Copy possibilities

In order to save unnecessary input work, Lotus 1-2-3 provides the possibility of copying the contents of cells. This may be done with texts, numbers and formulas.

With *texts and numbers* an exact duplication is made of the original data for another cell or cells. This can be interesting when make separation lines such as underlining.

If you wish to copy *formulas*, it is possible for the program to adjust the cell addresses automatically. It is important here to specify the cell addresses correctly and you must keep in mind the difference between relative, absolute and mixed cell addresses.

When copying, you make use of the Copy command in the main menu. Before giving the command, it is useful to go with the cell pointer to the cell to be copied or to the outermost cell, a corner, of a range. Subsequently, having selected the Copy command, the source and target range must be specified. After confirmation using Enter, the program will copy the specified range to the desired target range.

If you are working in windows with various worksheets (more about this later), you can copy from one worksheet window to another. When asked to specify the target range, in this case you must press F6 to be able to specify the target in another window.

2.6.2   Copying formulas

It is useful to be able to copy a formula if the same calculation has to made repeatedly in a certain row or column.

In our example dealing with turnover, it is advisable, for example, to enter the formula in cell C4 first and to copy it from there to the cells C5 to C15. The calculation of the percentage in the turnover remains the same for each month. Thus, it is not necessary to enter the formula in each individual cell.

First, the formula has to be constructed in cell C4 for the month of January. This is as follows:

```
+B4*100/B17
```

The screen should then look like this:

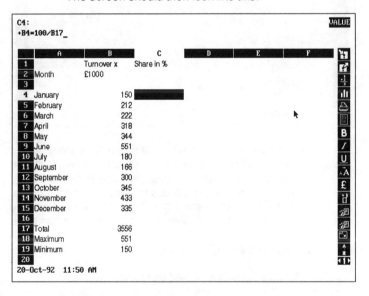

When the command has been confirmed, the screen will look like this:

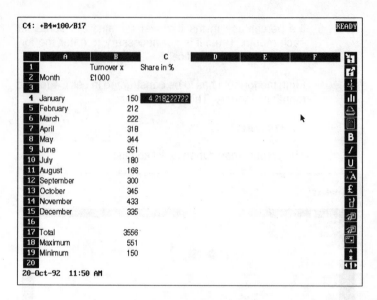

You will observe that the result displays as many places behind the decimal point as the column width allows. The formula which has been entered in cell C4 must now be copied eleven times for the remaining months. To do this, we choose the Copy command from the main menu using /C. When the source range has been specified (Copy what?), you can specify the destination range (To where?): C5 to C15.

Thus, a formula is copied as follows:

■ Using the cursor keys, activate the cell which is to be copied.
■ Select the Copy command from the main menu using /C.
■ Specify the source range and confirm this using Enter.
■ Do the same for the destination range.
■ When you have confirmed this using Enter, the formula will be copied.

The following screen is the result:

```
C4:  +B4*100/B17                                                    READY

        A           B           C           D         E         F
 1               Turnover x   Share in %
 2  Month        £1000
 3
 4  January           150    4.218222722
 5  February          212    38.47549909
 6  March             222        148
 7  April             318        ERR
 8  May               344        ERR
 9  June              551        ERR
10  July              180        ERR
11  August            166        ERR
12  September         300        ERR
13  October           345        ERR
14  November          433        ERR
15  December          335        ERR
16
17  Total            3556
18  Maximum           551
19  Minimum           150
20
20-Oct-92  11:51 AM
```

The figure shows that we have made an error some-
where. This is due to the fact that we have not taken into
consideration the difference between absolute and
relative addresses. In principle, Lotus addresses the
cells in a relative way when the cell pointer is used. This
means that, when copying, the cell position is always
determined relative to the copy direction. The relative
cell address is correct for the cell in which the turnover
is located. In this way, when copying the formula, the
cells for the subsequent months, B5 , B6 etc. are addressed. The total turnover, the sum, in cell B17 is different. The reference point of the formula, in the
example, must always be exactly cell B17. This cell address must not move downwards as it does when the
turnover cells are addressed. The corresponding
monthly turnover must be compared to B17. Accordingly, B17 must be addressed absolutely. To do this, it is
necessary to enter a dollar sign before the specification
of the column and row B17. The formula will then appear as follows:

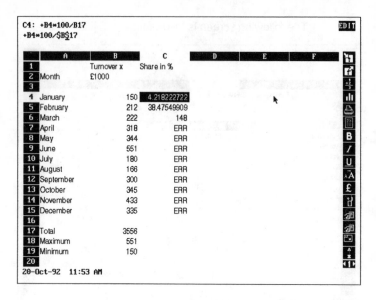

Lotus 1-2-3 always addresses cells relatively, in principle. The address becomes absolute only when the
dollar sign is specified. For those who find it too much
work to specify the dollar signs, there is an alternative.
When the appropriate cell has been activated using the
cell pointer, you only need to activate the ABS function
using the function key F4. In this way, an absolute address is specified. This function can be cancelled by
pressing F4 once more.

absolute cell address	**relative cell address**
the cell address in the copy must correspond to the original	the cell address is deter-mined by the relative posi-tion
the sum, in our example	the monthly turnover, in our example
$B$17	B4

If you now repeat the Copy command, the screen will appear as follows:

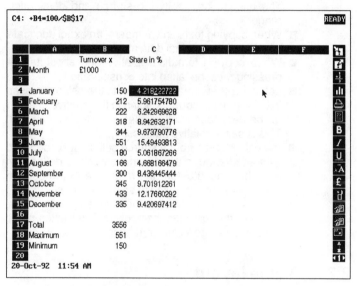

Finally, save this table under the name TURNOVR2.

In fact, when the annual turnover was addressed, only the row needed to be addressed absolutely. The column could have retained its relative address. Thus, the dollar sign in front of the B was not really necessary. In this case, we are dealing with a combined address, since only one of the factors, column or row, receives a dollar sign. In our example the result still remains the same. However, there is an advantage to mixed reference. For instance, if we should add a column containing real turnover values, this formula could be copied directly.

2.6.3 Summary of section 2.6

■ Copying cell data saves a great deal of unnecessary work.

- Texts, numbers and formulas can be copied.
- Cell data can be copied using the Copy command. The user must specify the source and destination range.
- When copying texts and numbers, an exact duplicate is made of the original data at another position.
- When copying formulas, relative and absolute addressing must be taken into consideration.
- Lotus 1-2-3 automatically adjusts the cell addresses in the formulas, corresponding to the relative position of the destination cell in relation to the source cell. This is called relative addressing.
- If a cell address from a source cell must be adopted without change in the destination cell, a dollar sign must be placed before the reference to the column and/or row. This is called absolute addressing.
- It is also possible to copy the values of formulas instead of the formulas themselves. That takes place using the Range Value command.

2.7   Table layout

The previous figure shows that the calculated percentages are displayed as precisely as possible, depending on the column width. However, this is not always orderly or necessary. The format can be altered if required. This also applies to the layout of the cell data.

2.7.1   Aligning cell data

As previously mentioned, Lotus 1-2-3 left-aligns the labels (texts) in the cells and right-aligns the numbers. As we have seen, this layout can be altered using the Worksheet Global Format command.

However, this can be done specifically for certain cells in a worksheet. The possibilities are Left, Right and Center. To do this, select the Range Label submenu in which you can specify the appropriate range and required option. In our example, we shall right-align the

text data in columns B and C in order to have them align
with the number values in these columns. Proceed as
follows:

■ Activate the first cell using the cursor keys.
■ Select the Range Label submenu using /RL.
■ Select the layout option using the cursor keys.
■ Specify the appropriate range using the cursor keys.
■ Confirm using Enter.

The result is shown in the following figure. The text data
in the specified range are now aligned to the numbers
underneath:

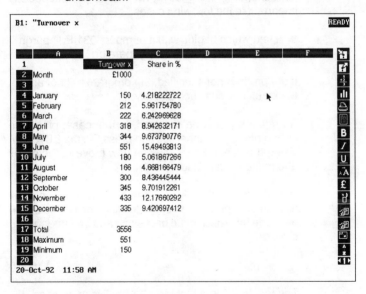

You will have noticed that each text label in the Control
Panel is supplied with a prefix. This prefix refers to the
way in which the text is aligned. In our example, inverted commas are located where the apostrophe used
to be up until now. The meaning of the various prefixes:

sign	meaning
' apostrophe	left-aligned
" inverted commas	right-aligned
^ caret	centred
\ backslash	repeat

If you wish to have a different form of alignment than normal, you can specify the appropriate sign when making the input. This is not reproduced in the cell itself in the worksheet. It is only shown on the first line of the Control Panel when the cell pointer is located in the corresponding cell. Placing a format sign is especially important in the following cases:

- a text which begins with a number: '031 Edinburgh
- a text which begins with an operator: '+17.5% VAT.

If the prefix is not specified, the program will not accept the input in cases such as these.

A prefix may also be changed. In that case, place the cell pointer on the label cell and press F2, the EDIT key. Using the cursor keys, you can now move to the prefix and make the alteration.

Use of the backslash is very handy if characters in a cell have to be repeated. An extended line, for example, can be made by pressing the backslash and one underlining sign:

The result of this is that the whole cell is underlined.

2.7.2 Specifying the format code and the number of decimal places

In a previous example, we have seen that it is possible to have a large amount of figures behind the decimal point. Fifteen is the maximum. The number format can

also be changed, although the format does not influence the number stored in the Lotus 1-2-3 memory.
The internal accuracy remains the same regardless of
the display on screen.

In order to change the number format to two digits behind the point, you should proceed as follows: select the
Range Format submenu. You are then able to choose
from the following options:

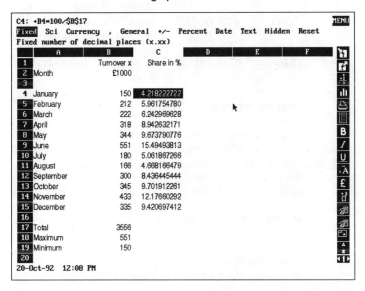

The options have the following significance:

format	example	function
Fixed	4.2	fixed number of digits (here 1) behind the decimal point, maximum of 15
Sci	-4.3E+01	exponential, scientific notation
Currency	£9.99	adds currency symbol to the value (in front or behind)

Comma	1,000	thousands separator
General	4,178	real numbers, meaning-less zeroes behind the de-cimal point omitted
+/-	++++++	symbol display (bar chart)
Percent	4.178%	adds percent sign
Date	10/11	various (5) methods of dis-playing the date
Time	20:00	various (4) methods of dis-playing the time
Text	+C5-D5	displays the formula as text not as calculated value
Hidden		suppresses display of data
Reset		restores the standard set-tings

We shall return to the date and time settings later.

In our example, we wish to limit the percentages to one digit behind the decimal point. To do this, the format set-ting for the cells containing the percentages should be altered using the Fixed option in the submenu. In order to change the format of cell C4, proceed as follows:

- Using the cursor keys, place the cell pointer on the first cell.
- Select the Range Format submenu using /RF.
- Select the Fixed option by pressing Enter.
- Specify the number of digits behind the decimal point: 1.
- Press Enter
- Confirm the range to be formatted by pressing Enter.

2.7.3   Formatting ranges

Individual formatting of each cell is very laborious if the intention is to format a group of cells (a row or column). Accordingly, Lotus 1-2-3 provides the possibility of marking a range, after the number of digits behind the decimal point has been specified. This saves a great deal of work in situations like these. Being able to specify ranges makes working with spreadsheets a good deal easier. Often when a command has been activated, the program will request specification of the relevant range.

In this context, range refers to a rectangular block of cells which belong together. This can be:

■ a part of a column
■ a part of a row
■ a block containing several rows and columns.

There are various ways of specifying a range in Lotus 1-2-3:

■ by specifying the cell addresses. This means the cell in the top left-hand corner and that in the lower right-hand corner, separated from each other by two points.
■ by activating the cells using the cell pointer. Using the cell pointer, move to the first corner cell and anchor it by pressing the full-stop key. Then go to the second corner cell, the end of the range. Press Enter to confirm the extent of the range. With some commands the beginning cells are automatically anchored.
■ by using range names (more about this later).

The formatting procedure for the range is thus as follows:

■ Using the cursor keys, place the cell pointer on the beginning cell.
■ Select the Range Format submenu using /RF.
■ Select the Fixed option by pressing Enter.
■ Specify the number of digits behind the decimal point: 1
■ Specify the range by moving the cursor keys over the required cells.
■ Confirm the values entered by pressing Enter.

The result of this formatting is that the percentages in the third column of the table retain only one digit behind the decimal point:

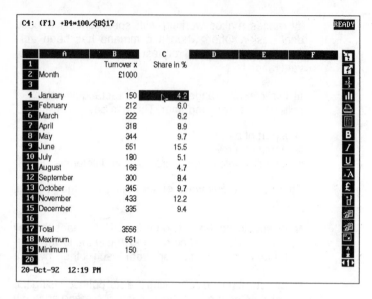

Save the table under the name TURNOVR2.

2.7.4   Summary of section 2.7

■ Cell data are formatted according to the standard settings or according to the specifications applied using
Worksheet Global. Using commands from the Range
submenu, local alterations can be made.

■ Using the Range Label command, individual cells or
specified ranges containing text data can be aligned
differently. The options are Left, Right and Center.

■ The method of alignment can also be determined at
the input of the data, by placing a prefix sign.

■ Using the Range Format submenu, number values
can be displayed in different notation.

2.8   Editing and extending tables

Various situations may make it necessary to edit an existing table. This may require the following manoeuvres:

- adding rows or columns
- removing rows or columns
- relocating rows or columns
- altering cell data.

Exercise 2-3: Editing tables

Extend the table in our example to include real turnover values alongside the estimated values. In addition, another column should be included to show the difference between the estimated and the real turnover.

The final result should appear as follows (the table should be saved under the name TURNOVR3):

Month	Estimated Turnover x £1000	Share in %	Real Turnover x £1000	Share in %	Difference Est.-Real x £1000
January	150	4.2	132	3.9	-18
February	212	6.0	260	7.6	48
March	222	6.2	322	9.4	100
April	318	8.9	312	9.2	-6
May	344	9.7	322	9.4	-22
June	551	15.5	457	13.4	-94
July	180	5.1	234	6.9	54
August	166	4.7	239	7.0	73
September	300	8.4	234	6.9	-66
October	345	9.7	317	9.3	-28
November	433	12.2	345	10.1	-88
December	335	9.4	234	6.9	-101
Total	3556		3408		
Maximum	551		457		
Minimum	150		132		

2.8.1   Adding rows and columns

If a table has to be edited at a later date, it may occur that extra rows or columns have to be added. Space can be created in the table for extra data.

We shall edit the table TURNOVR2. This is loaded using the File Retrieve command.

Adding rows

To include the proper titles above the columns, a new row must be added at the top of the table. Place the cell pointer at the position where the new row is to come (A1). Then select the Worksheet Insert Row command. When the command has been confirmed by pressing Enter, the worksheet will appear as shown in the figure below:

```
A1:                                                                    READY

          A           B           C           D           E           F

 1
 2                  Turnover x    Share in %
 3   Month            £1000
 4
 5   January           150          4.2
 6   February          212          6.0
 7   March             222          6.2
 8   April             318          8.9
 9   May               344          9.7
10   June              551         15.5
11   July              180          5.1
12   August            166          4.7
13   September         300          8.4
14   October           345          9.7
15   November          433         12.2
16   December          335          9.4
17
18   Total            3556
19   Maximum           551
20   Minimum           150
20-Oct-92   12:23 PM
```

Now the former table can be supplemented with new data:

■ text data in the rows 1-3
■ the real figures are placed in column D
■ formulas are placed in columns E and F.

This action and the addition of data produces the following screen (note the right-aligned columns):

	A	B	C	D	E	F	
		Estimated		Real		Difference	
1		Turnover x	Share in %	Turnover x	Share in %	Est.–Real x	
2		£1000		£1000		£1000	
3	Month						
4							
5	January	150	4.2	132	3.9	−18	
6	February	212	6.0	260	7.6	48	
7	March	222	6.2	322	9.4	100	
8	April	318	8.9	312	9.2	−6	
9	May	344	9.7	322	9.4	−22	
10	June	551	15.5	457	13.4	−94	
11	July	180	5.1	234	6.9	54	
12	August	166	4.7	239	7.0	73	
13	September	300	8.4	234	6.9	−66	
14	October	345	9.7	317	9.3	−28	
15	November	433	12.2	345	10.1	−88	
16	December	335	9.4	234	6.9	−101	
17	-------						
18	Total	3556		3408			
19	Maximum	551		457			
20	Minimum	150		132			

A1:   READY

20-Oct-92 12:31 PM

Now save the worksheet under the name TURNOVR3.

Adding columns

Columns are added in the same way as rows. To acquaint yourself with the possibilities, select the Worksheet Insert Column command. By pressing Esc, you will return to the worksheet.

In general, the insertion of columns takes place as follows:

■ using the cursor keys, place the cell pointer on the first cell

■ select the Worksheet Insert submenu using /WI
■ select Column, press Enter
■ specify the number of columns using the cursor keys
■ conclude the command by pressing Enter.

Of course, it is also possible to delete columns or rows later. To do this, use the Worksheet Delete command.

2.8.2   Moving rows

Using the Move command, the contents of cells or cell ranges can be moved to another position in the table. Proceed as follows:

■ Using the cursor keys, activate the initial cell (corner cell to be moved).
■ Select the Move instruction using /M.
■ Specify the source range using the cursor keys (or type when requested).
■ Specify the destination range using the cursor keys (or type when requested).
■ Confirm using Enter.

When the command has been executed, the cells are located at a different position in the worksheet. The original contents of any cells in the destination area are removed during this operation. Formulas in moved cells are automatically adjusted. Thus, the functional relationships between the cells is retained.

2.8.3   Altering cell input

If number values are altered, the relevant cells are automatically recalculated. You can check this, for instance, by altering the estimation for the month of June from 551 to 777. The following table is the result:

B10: 777   READY

A	B	C	D	E	F
	Estimated		Real		Difference
	Turnover x	Share in %	Turnover x	Share in %	Est.−Real x
3 Month	£1000		£1000		£1000
4					
5 January	150	4.0	132	3.9	−18
6 February	212	5.6	260	7.6	48
7 March	222	5.9	322	9.4	100
8 April	318	8.4	312	9.2	−6
9 May	344	9.1	322	9.4	−22
10 June	777	20.5	457	13.4	−320
11 July	180	4.8	234	6.9	54
12 August	166	4.4	239	7.0	73
13 September	300	7.9	234	6.9	−66
14 October	345	9.1	317	9.3	−28
15 November	433	11.4	345	10.1	−88
16 December	335	8.9	234	6.9	−101
17					
18 Total	3782		3408		
19 Maximum	777		457		
20 Minimum	150		132		

20−Oct−92 12:32 PM

The figure shows that all related values have been re-calculated. These are:

■ in column B, the total value at Total and the Maximum value
■ all values in column C
■ the difference between estimated and real turnover in cell F10.

2.8.4   Summary of section 2.8

■ Rows and columns can be inserted into the table later. This takes place using the Worksheet Insert command.
■ Using the Worksheet Delete command, rows and columns can be removed later.
■ The contents of a cell range can be moved to another part of the table using the Move command.
■ If new number values are introduced into a cell, Lotus 1-2-3 recalculates the values for all related cells.

2.9   Printing Lotus tables

We shall now commit the above saved table to paper. In principle, the printout should conform to the display on the screen. This applies to both the specified column width and the layout of the cell data (alignment of texts and numeric display formats).

Often, special demands are made upon the printout of a table, for example:

- Not the whole table, but only a part if it is to be printed.
- Documentation objectives require the formulas to be printed instead of the calculated values.
- To make the table clearer, the printed table should be allocated a certain text in a header or footer.

We shall deal with the printing procedure and a number of variations using the following example:

Exercise 2-4: Printing Lotus tables

Load the table TURNOVR3.WK1 and specify the following variations for printing:

(a)   Print the table on the installed printer exactly as shown on the screen.

(b)   Subsequently print the formulas from the table.

(c)   Finally, the table should be printed with the header 'Turnover Analysis 1992; Shylock Ltd.'.

2.9.1   Standard settings for printing

Printing tables in Lotus 1-2-3 takes place via the Print command from the main menu. When you have selected this option, you will see that it is possible to transport the table not only directly to the printer but also to a file. In the latter case, it is then possible to print the file from DOS, or to use it in another program, for example a word-processing program.

To send the table to the printer, select the Print Printer command. However, it is advisable to check the parameters beforehand, especially if this is the first time you are printing something from Lotus 1-2-3. First go to the Worksheet Global Default Printer menu. The following screen will appear:

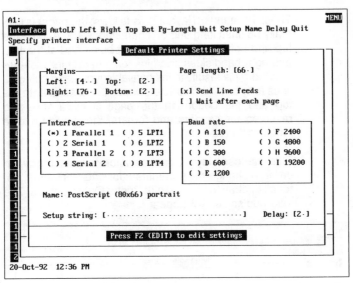

The following parameters are especially important here:

Page length   The default setting is 66 lines. This can be defined to any amount between 1 and 100.

Left   The options for the left and right margins determine the amount of characters printed per line. The standard setting in Lotus is a left margin of four characters.

Right   This determines the right-hand margin. Normally, this begins at line position 76, so that 72 characters can be placed on a line.

Top   This determines how large the upper margin should be. Normally, two blank lines are printed.

Bottom   Normally, two blank lines are also placed at the bottom of the page.

Thus, the standard layout is as follows: the paper is normally 66 lines long and 80 characters wide. At both the top and bottom, two lines are left blank and at the left- and right-hand sides, margins four characters wide are created. This results in the available type page being 62 lines long and 72 characters wide. Because at both the top and the bottom of the page 3 extra lines are reserved for headers and footers, the resulting page length is 56 (62-6).

This standard layout can be altered quite easily. In order to change the parameters for one worksheet, not for all (global), go to the Print Printer Options menu. The following screen will appear:

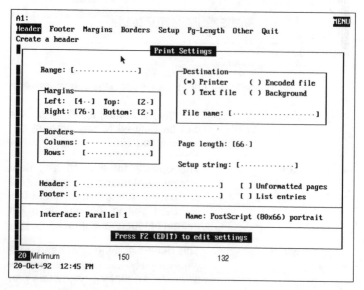

Using margins and Pg-Length you may choose other settings if required.

2.9.2 Starting the print procedure

First check if the printer is ready and supplied with paper. To start the print procedure, go to work as follows:

■ Activate the submenu Print Printer using /PP.
■ Select the Range option using R.
■ Go to the first cell and anchor it by pressing the full-stop key.
■ Using the cursor keys, go to a corner cell.

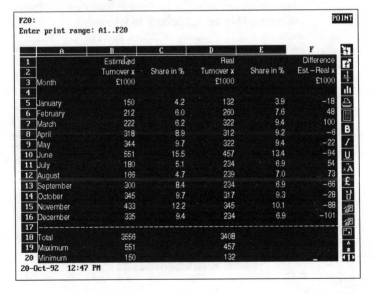

■ Press Enter.
■ Select Options or Margins if required.
■ Start printing by selecting Go.

The table will be subsequently printed on the installed printer. If problems arise during printing, the print procedure can be discontinued by pressing the Break key. It is important that a text printer has been specified during the installation, otherwise an error message will appear. You can leave the Print submenu via Quit.

2.9.3 Printing a table with the corresponding formulas

Normally, the results of the formulas in a table are trans-ported to the screen or printer. But sometimes it may be extremely useful to print the cells with their formulas to check the structure of the table, for instance, or for doc-umentation objectives.

This can be regulated in the Print Printer Options Other submenu. This menu appears as follows:

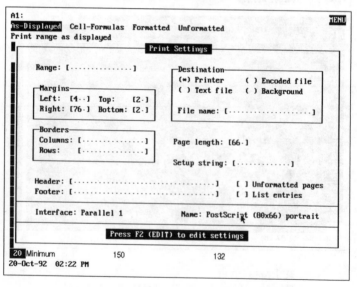

Select the Cell-Formulas option. This enables you to make the desired printout of the worksheet with the for-mulas.

The procedure is as follows:

- Activate the Print Printer submenu using /PP.
- Select the Options Other command using OO.
- Select the Cell-Formulas option using C.
- Return to the Print menu using Esc.
- Start printing using Go.

The following printout is the result:

```
B1: "Estimated
D1: "Real
F1: "Difference
B2: "Turnover x
C2: "Share in %
D2: "Turnover x
E2: "Share in %
F2: "Est.-Real x
A3: 'Month
B3: (C0) "£1000
D3: "£1000
F3: "£1000
A5: 'January
B5: 150
C5: (F1) +B5*100/$B$18
D5: 132
E5: (F1) +D5*100/$D$18
F5: +D5-B5
A6: 'February
B6: 212
C6: (F1) +B6*100/$B$18
D6: 260
E6: (F1) +D6*100/$D$18
F6: +D6-B6
A7: 'March
B7: 222
C7: (F1) +B7*100/$B$18
D7: 322
E7: (F1) +D7*100/$D$18
F7: +D7-B7
A8: 'April
B8: 318
C8: (F1) +B8*100/$B$18
D8: 312
```

```
E8: (F1) +D8*100/$D$18
F8: +D8-B8
A9: 'May
B9: 344
C9: (F1) +B9*100/$B$18
D9: 322
E9: (F1) +D9*100/$D$18
F9: +D9-B9
A10: 'June
B10: 551
C10: (F1) +B10*100/$B$18
D10: 457
E10: (F1) +D10*100/$D$18
F10: +D10-B10
A11: 'July
B11: 180
C11: (F1) +B11*100/$B$18
D11: 234
E11: (F1) +D11*100/$D$18
F11: +D11-B11
A12: 'August
B12: 166
C12: (F1) +B12*100/$B$18
D12: 239
E12: (F1) +D12*100/$D$18
F12: +D12-B12
A13: 'September
B13: 300
C13: (F1) +B13*100/$B$18
D13: 234
E13: (F1) +D13*100/$D$18
F13: +D13-B13
A14: 'October
B14: 345
C14: (F1) +B14*100/$B$18
D14: 317
E14: (F1) +D14*100/$D$18
F14: +D14-B14
A15: 'November
B15: 433
C15: (F1) +B15*100/$B$18
D15: 345
```

```
E15:  (F1) +D15*100/$D$18
F15:  +D15-B15
A16:  'December
B16:  335
C16:  (F1) +B16*100/$B$18
D16:  234
E16:  (F1) +D16*100/$D$18
F16:  +D16-B16
A17:  \-
B17:  \-
C17:  \-
D17:  \-
E17:  \-
F17:  \-
A18:  'Total
B18:  @SUM(B5..B16)
D18:  @SUM(D5..D16)
A19:  'Maximum
B19:  @MAX(B5..B16)
D19:  @MAX(D5..D16)
A20:  'Minimum
B20:  @MIN(B5..B16)
D20:  @MIN(D5..D16)
```

As you will observe, a list is printed with the entire contents of all cells in the worksheet. Instead of values, the formulas are shown. In addition, in each row the cell address, the format and the protection status, if any, are displayed.

2.9.4   Printing a table with headers and footers

Lotus 1-2-3 provides the possibility of printing tables with headers and footers. This is especially useful in cases of tables which consist of several pages. In our example, we are dealing with the header 'Turnover analysis; Shylock Ltd.'.

In addition, it is very useful to have page numeration for tables which consist of more than one page. To do this, a number sign (#) must be placed in the header or footer. This determines that the numeration should be consecutive, beginning at number 1.

Proceed as follows:

- Activate the Print Printer submenu using /PP.
- Select Options using O.
- Select the Header option using H.
- Enter the appropriate text ('Turnover Analysis....) and press Enter.
- Return to the Print menu using Quit - press Q.

The header text is printed just under the top edge of each page. The maximum length of the text is 240 characters, depending on the specified width of the paper.

2.9.5 Printing parts of a table

Occasionally, it is useful to be able to print only a part of a table. This is also possible in Lotus 1-2-3 and takes place using the Print Printer Range command in which the required range can be specified (for example A1..C20).

2.9.6 Changing letter type and size

It can also be useful to print a table in a compressed form in order to squeeze more columns onto a page and thus increase the reference survey. This is possible using the Print Printer Options command where you can select the Setup option.

Here you are able to specify a number of operating characters for the printer. For this, the operating codes of the installed printer are necessary. Consult the printer manual. You will find the corresponding conversions in the Lotus 1-2-3 supplement supplied with the package.

The following codes apply to many printers:

desired effect	code
compressed printing	\015
non-compressed printing	\018
8 lines per inch	\270
6 lines per inch	\0272

Pay attention to the following when specifying a code:

■ A backslash must be placed in front of the actual code.
■ The code follows, consisting of three or four numbers.
■ A code which has been previously specified can be removed using the Esc key.

If you are making a compressed printout, a maximum of 132 characters per line can be used on paper which has a standard width of 80 pica characters.

2.9.7 Printing a table with horizontal or vertical titles

Tables which consist of several pages should have the same border or header. This can be specified in the Print Printer Options Borders menu. This enables certain lines or columns to be printed on each page above or to the left of the specified range. In the submenu, a certain range must be specified in the Rows and Columns options.

2.9.8 Summary of section 2.9

■ Tables can be printed using the submenu Print. In addition to a direct printout of the desired table, certain options can be specified.
■ The standard setting for the print menu is located in the Worksheet Global Default submenu.
■ Special print options can be specified, in special cases, using the Print Printer Options submenu.
■ Before printing begins, a range must be specified

using Print Printer Range. Then start printing using the Go command.

■ Other possibilities are:
  – printing formulas using Print Printer Options Other
  – printing tables with headers and footers
  – compressed printing
  – duplication of titles in the case of tables which consist of several pages.

2.10   Using range names with formulas

Use of range names can be important when constructing formulas, especially with large tables. Instead of dull coordinates, names can be entered. Reference to particular cells or cell ranges becomes simpler. In addition, it is easier to make links to other tables and to tranfer number values to the graphic mode.

Exercise 2-5: Assigning range names in Lotus tables

Load the table TURNOVR2.WK1. Using this table, we shall examine how names are assigned and how they are used in the application of formulas. Execute the following instructions:

Allocate the following ranges the corresponding name:

■ The range B4..B15 should be called 'Turnover'.
■ The range C4..C15 should be called 'Share'.

Subsequently, using the name 'Share' in the addition formula in cell C17.

Save the table under the name TURNOVR4.

In Lotus 1-2-3, names are assigned using Range Name. The submenu appears as follows:

```
B4: 150                                                              MENU
Create  Delete  Labels  Reset  Table
Create or modify a range name
        A              B            C         D         E         F
 1                 Turnover x    Share in %
 2  Month            £1000
 3
 4  January            150          4.2
 5  February           212          6.0
 6  March              222          6.2
 7  April              3?8          8.9
 8  May                344          9.7
 9  June               551         15.5
10  July               180          5.1
11  August             166          4.7
12  September          300          8.4
13  October            345          9.7
14  November           433         12.2
15  December           335          9.4
16
17  Total             3556
18  Maximum            551
19  Minimum            150
20
20-Oct-92  04:09 PM
```

The options have the following significance:

option   significance

Create   create or modify a range name
Delete   delete a range name
Label   use existing labels as range name
Reset   remove all range names from the table
Table   create a table with all range names and ad-
              dresses

Proceed as follows when assigning range names:

■ Activate the starting point using the cursor keys.
■ Select the Range Name Create submenu using
  /RNC.
■ Specify the range name 'Turnover'.
■ Specify the range up to B15.
■ Confirm using Enter.

Before confirmation, the screen will look like this:

```
B15: 335                                                              POINT
Enter name: Turnover                    Enter range: B4..B15
```

	A	B	C	D	E	F
1		Turnover x	Share in %			
2	Month	£1000				
3						
4	January	150	4.2			
5	February	212	6.0			
6	March	222	6.2			
7	April	318	8.9			
8	May	344	9.7			
9	June	551	15.5			
10	July	180	5.1			
11	August	166	4.7			
12	September	300	8.4			
13	October	345	9.7			
14	November	433	12.2			
15	December	335	9.4			
16						
17	Total	3556				
18	Maximum	551				
19	Minimum	150				
20						

```
20-Oct-92  04:13 PM
```

Pay attention to the following rules when specifying a name:

■ Names must begin with a letter.
■ Names may not contain spaces or hyphens.
■ Letters, numbers, periods and underlining are permitted.

Now assign the name 'Share' to the range C4..C15. When you have implemented this instruction, you will observe that the range names are already applied to the existing formulas in B17, B18 and B19. Place the cell pointer on B17 and this will be evident. In the Control Panel area at the top of the screen, the following formula is shown:

```
@SUM(TURNOVER)
```

You can now do the same for the sum formula for the share. Go to cell C17 and enter the following formula:

```
@SUM(SHARE)
```

When you have implemented the instruction, the following will appear on the screen:

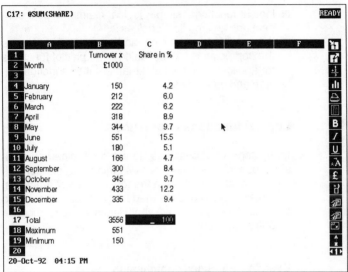

If, when constructing a formula, you have forgotten which name you have allocated to a range, you can request a list of range names by pressing the NAME key (F3) when in the Range menu.

In summary, working with range names is particularly interesting when references to a certain range are frequently made in a table. The name of a range, if carefully chosen, is easier to apply in formulas than exact addressing by means of the cursor keys or cell coordinates.

2.11 Special functions in worksheet calculations

As mentioned, Lotus 1-2-3 provides a large number of functions which help simplify working with the program.

We shall deal with some of these functions in this section. These include:

- logical functions: simple logical claims, logical connections and multiple choices
- the capital value function and functions to calculate the depreciation values, being examples of functions for application of financial-mathematical functions
- time and date functions.

2.11.1   Logical functions in practice

Many aspects of business life are determined by decisions based on variable data. In this area, the spreadsheet provides services in the form of logical functions. Complex applications are made more accessible. Using the following exercise, we shall describe the application of logical functions.

Exercise 2-6: Sales commission

The following Lotus worksheet must calculate the commission of the salesmen in a company. A commission of 5% of the annual turnover is available if the turnover is greater than £400,000. Otherwise a fixed sum of £10,000 will be paid. The worksheet should appear as follows:

Calculation of the commission per salesman

Name	Annual turnover	Commission
Bogart	£350,000.00	£10,000.00
Delon	£345,776.00	£10,00000
Olivier	£890,655.00	£44,532.75
Caine	£660,000.00	£33,000.00
Connery	£390,000.00	£10,000.00
Cagney	£1,450,000.00	£72,500.00
Gans	£560,000.00	£28,000.00
Reagan	£177,999.00	£10,00.00

Dean	£378,000.00	£10,000.00
Total	£5,202,430.00	£228,032.75

Notes:
- The width of all columns should be 24.
- The worksheet should be saved under the name COMMISSN.

The special feature of this worksheet is the calculation of the commission sum. In order to make this, the worksheet should be constructed in the following stages:

- The column width should be set to the standard width of 24 characters by specifying the number 24 in the submenu Worksheet Global Column Width.
- Enter the title in the first row.
- Enter text in column A, number values in column B. Underlining should be done in rows 4 and 14.
- Enter the sum formula in cell B15:

```
@SUM(B5..B13)
```

- Specify the number values displaying the currency symbol and a comma separator for thousands using the Worksheet Global Format Currency menu.

In the calculation of the commission, we must make use of the function IF. The syntax of this function is:

```
@IF(condition,x,y)
```

The condition is examined during calculation of the cell in question. If the condition is seen to be TRUE, then the result is *x*, otherwise it is *y*. In the example the condition is B5>400000. If this condition is satisfied, then the calculation is *x*:B5*0.05. Otherwise it is *y*:10000.

Thus, the formula in C5 should be:

```
@IF(B5>400000,B5*0.05,10000)
```

When you have entered all this, the following screen will
appear:

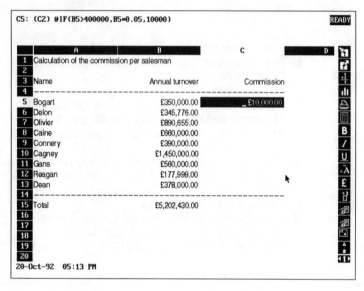

The formula in C5 can be copied to the cells C6 to C13
using the Copy command. The result should produce
the desired worksheet.

Logical functions can also be linked to each other, so
that multiple claims are possible. The general syntax is:

```
@IF(condition,x,@IF(condition,x,y))
```

This formula can be extended at will. Keep in mind
when constructing a formula like this that the number of
opening brackets coincides with the number of closing
brackets.

We shall apply this in practice in the following example.

Exercise 2-7: Break-even analysis

In this example, we shall make a break-even analysis. The calculation of the profit threshold is an important aid when deciding if your proposed new product should actually be brought into production. The worksheet which we shall make provides a model for this application. Keep the following steps in mind:

- First enter the data under the name Data.
- Then specify the formulas in a way that they can easily be copied downwards.
- Save the file under the name BREAK.

Data:			
Returns per article	360		
Var. cost/article	152		
Abs. fixed costs	50000		
Var. fixed costs	30000	Initial amount	850
Amount interval	500	Analysis interval	25

Calculation and analysis:

Amount	Returns	Var. costs costs	Abs. fixed costs	Var. fixed costs	Total	Profit
850	306000	129200	50000	60000	239200	66800
875	315000	133000	50000	60000	243000	72000
900	324000	136800	50000	60000	246800	77200
925	333000	140600	50000	60000	250600	82400
950	342000	144400	50000	60000	254400	87600
975	351000	148200	50000	60000	258200	92800
1000	360000	152000	50000	90000	292000	68000
1025	369000	155800	50000	90000	295800	73200
1050	378000	159600	50000	90000	299600	78400
1075	387000	163400	50000	90000	303400	83600
1100	396000	167200	50000	90000	307200	88800
1125	405000	171000	50000	90000	311000	94000
1150	414000	174800	50000	90000	314800	99200
1175	423000	178600	50000	90000	318600	104400
1200	432000	182400	50000	90000	322400	109600
1225	441000	186200	50000	90000	326200	114800
1250	450000	190000	50000	90000	330000	120000
1275	459000	193800	50000	90000	333800	125200
1300	468000	197600	50000	90000	337600	130400

In the example, there are seven separate fields for data in the upper part. With regard to these fields, calculations are made in the lower part. Here, taking a random amount, an analysis of any situation can be made.

The formulas in the lower part must be constructed in such a way that they can be applied to the rows below using the Copy command. In the columns of the first row (row 14), we find the following construction of the diverse formulas:

(1)   Calculation of the amount (column 1): as initial amount, the number in cell G6 is adopted in A14 (+G6), and then the following formula is applied to cell A15: previous cell + analysis interval. In

addition, the addressing of cell A14 must be relative, while the reference to the value of the analysis interval must be absolute. For cell A15, this means:

```
+A14+$G$7
```

Subsequently, the other cells receive this formula via Copy.

(2) Calculation of the returns (column B): the returns are calculated by multiplying the amount of articles by the returns per article. Here, the field dealing with the quantity should be addressed relatively and the field for the returns per article absolutely. An example:

```
+A14*$C$3
```

(3) Variable costs (column C): the variable costs are calculated by multiplying the quantity by the variable costs per article. Example:

```
+A14*$C$4
```

(4) Absolute overhead costs (column D): are adopted from field C5 (+$C$5). Subsequently, copy downwards.

(5) Variable overheads (column E): in order to calculate the variable overheads, it is necessary to request the appropriate quantity interval. Using the @IF function, a multiple of the staggered sums corresponding to the quantity interval can be calculated. In general, that should take place as follows:

```
@IF(amount<quant.interval,
var.overheads,@IF(amount<
quant.interval*2,var.overheads
*2,@IF(amount<quant.interval*3,
var.overheads*3,var.overheads*4)))
```

In our tangible example, that means the following for cell C14:

```
@IF(A14<$C$7,$C$6,@IF(A14<$C$7*2,$C$6
*2,@IF(A14<$C$7*3,$C$6*3,$C$6*4)))
```

(6)   Total costs: these are calculated by added up all the previous costs.

(7)   Profit: the profit is the difference between the returns and the total costs.

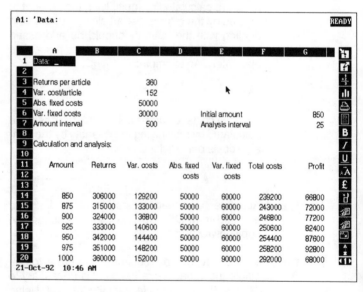

```
A21:  +A20+$G$7                                                    READY

        A          B          C         D        E        F         G
 21     1025    369000     155800     50000    90000    295800     73200
 22     1050    378000     159600     50000    90000    299600     78400
 23     1075    387000     163400     50000    90000    303400     83600
 24     1100    396000     167200     50000    90000    307200     88800
 25     1125    405000     171000     50000    90000    311000     94000
 26     1150    414000     174800     50000    90000    314800     99200
 27     1175    423000     178600     50000    90000    318600    104400
 28     1200    432000     182400     50000    90000    322400    109600
 29     1225    441000     186200     50000    90000    326200    114800
 30     1250    450000     190000     50000    90000    330000    120000
 31     1275    459000     193800     50000    90000    333800    125200
 32     1300    468000     197600     50000    90000    337600    130400
 33
 34
 35
 36
 37
 38
 39
 40
21-Oct-92  10:46 AM
```

The benefits of this model lie particularly in the flexible
application possibilities. Thus, with variations in the data
entered, alternative calculations can be carried out.

Briefly: as the examples show, the application area of
Lotus 1-2-3 can be extended by using logical functions.
The most important logical functions, which can also be
used in combination with each other are:

function   **significance**

@IF(condition,x,y)   if the condition is true, *x* is valid,
                      otherwise *y*.
@ERR   produces the logical value ERR
                      (value 0)
@ISERR(A)   if the argument in question, A, is an
                      ERR value, ISERR returns 1 (true).
@ISSTRING(A)   If argument A is a string, this will re-
                      turn the logical value 1 (true).
@ISNUMBER(A)   returns the true value (1) if the argu-
                      ment has a numeric value

2.11.2 Financial mathematical functions in practice

In various applications of financial mathematical work areas, spreadsheets provide a great number of functions which simplify financial and investment planning.
We shall deal with these functions in the light of two examples, one with a capital value function and one for the calculation of depreciation figures.

Exercise 2-8: Investment analysis using the capital value function

The following worksheet must calculate the profitability of an investment, based on the capital value method. The returns for the service life are placed opposite the total amount which is to be invested.

The following preconditions are important when constructing the worksheet:

- The total invested amount is placed in row 3.
- Row 4 contains the estimated service life in years. This is reckoned to be 10 years.
- The expected interest percentage is placed in row 5.
- The estimated returns (income) during the service life are entered in rows 8 to 17 inclusive. In the example, the income is estimated at £15,000 in the first year with an annual increase of 15%.
- The calculated capital value is placed in row 19.
- Finally, row 20 should show, by means of comparison of capital value and total investment, whether the investment is recommended.

Save the worksheet under the name CAPVALUE.

A value which is only achieved after several years has little significance today. The current value is called capital value in accounting jargon. Calculation of the capital value is called discount, in which an estimated interest percentage is taken into consideration. Accordingly, the forecast for the annual return is:

```
capital value = annual return/interest
factor
```

The interest factor is calculated using the formula:

$$(1 + p/100)^n$$

Here, *p* is the interest percentage and *n* is the number of years.

For the calculation of the capital value of annual returns over several years, Lotus 1-2-3 provides a function with the following syntax:

```
@NPV(interest,cash flow range)
```

Using this function, the capital value of the future returns resulting from a capital investment can be calculated. In this, the *interest* is taken to be a fixed percentage, while the concept *cash flow range* represents the range of estimated returns.

To solve this problem, we shall proceed as follows:

Structure of the worksheet

For the first column, the width should be increased to thirty characters using the Worksheet Column Width submenu. The second column should have a width of fifteen characters. Then enter the title of the worksheet and the other data.

Formulas to calculate the returns

First, in cell B8, the estimated returns of £15,000 for the first year should be entered. The returns have to be calculated separately in the cells B9..B12. The formula for this is as follows:

```
+B8*1.15
```

Due to the relative reference, it is possible to enter the formula in B9 alone and then to copy it to cells B10..B12.

Assigning the worksheet range a name

The range containing the returns values should receive a name. Activate first the initial field B8 and then the Range Name Create submenu. Assign the name 'Returns' and specify the range B8..B17.

Calculation of capital value

According to the exercise, the capital value should be entered in cell B19. We shall make use of the financial mathematical function which has the formula:

```
@NPV(B5/100,RETURNS)
```

Decision to invest

Finally, in cell B20, the conclusion whether or not to invest should be calculated. The formula is as follows:

```
@IF(B19>B3,"Yes","No")
```

In the formula, the text data 'Yes' and 'No' are registered as the result possibilities. Remember that when specifying the formula, text must be placed between inverted commas. When the instruction has been implemented, the required worksheet will appear. Save it under the name CAPVALUE.

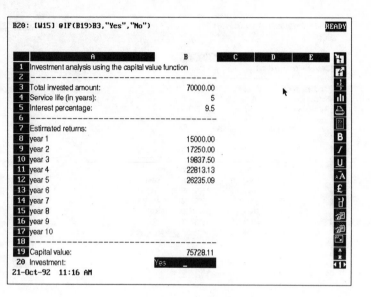

Exercise 2-9: Depreciation worksheet

Different depreciation methods should be displayed in a comparable survey. In this example, we shall begin with the following values:

- purchase price: £420,000
- service life: eight years
- residual (salvage) value: £20,000

This should produce the worksheet displayed below:

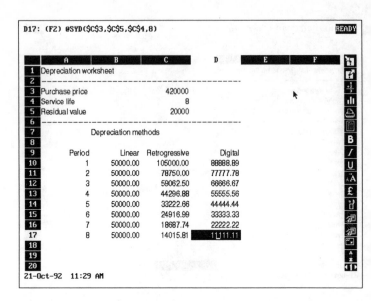

The global column width should be 12 characters. Save the worksheet under the name DEPRECN.

The financial mathematical functions of Lotus 1-2-3 are also used in this example. This concerns:

■ to calculate the linear depreciation:

`@SLN(cost,salvage,life)`

■ to calculate retrogressive depreciation:

`@DDB(cost,salvage,life,period)`

■ to calculate the sum-of-the-years'-digits depreciation:

`@SYD(cost,salvage,life,period)`

First create the basic worksheet. To do this, make the global column width 12 characters wide. Then enter the known data and values. This will produce the worksheet shown below.

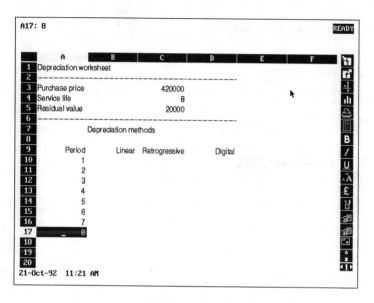

The formula for linear depreciation can now be constructed. First activate cell B10. The formula which is to be entered is as follows:

```
@SLN($C$3,$C$5,$C$4)
```

In this case, all values should be addressed absolutely. Because the values in each year are identical when dealing with linear depreciation, the formula in B10 can be directly copied down to cells B11..B17 using the Copy instruction from the main menu. This will produce the worksheet shown below.

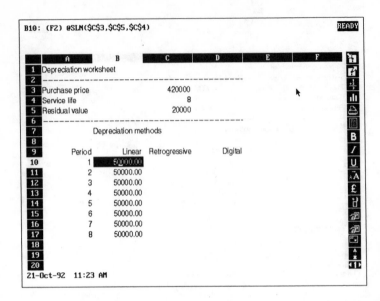

Now the formula for retrogressive depreciation can be placed in C10. The formula is as follows:

```
@DDB($C$3,$C$5,$C$4,1)
```

In the case of retrogressive depreciation, the formula cannot be directly copied to the other cells because the period repeatedly changes. Nevertheless, it is still possible to use the Copy instruction. This means that in each cell the corresponding period should be altered using the F2 key (EDIT mode), because the period is different in each case. This should produce the following worksheet. In addition, you must format the entire range in the fixed display style using two figures behind the decimal point (Worksheet Global Format Fixed).

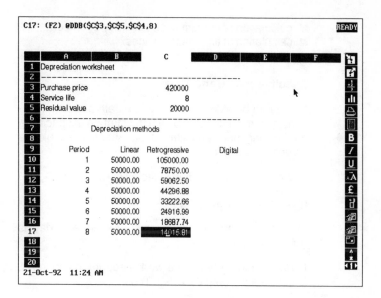

Digital depreciation is calculated in the same way as retrogressive depreciation. Enter the following formula in the D10 field:

```
@SYD($C$3,$C$5,$C$4,1)
```

After copying the formula and correcting the periods, the required worksheet should be complete. Finally, save the worksheet under the name DEPRECN.

You can learn more concerning the Lotus 1-2-3 financial mathematical functions by making use of the Help screen or by consulting the manual.

2.11.3 Date and time functions in practice

Lotus 1-2-3 supplies not only information about the date and time, it also has functions dealing with these. Useful applications of date and time functions in practice are:

■ effective control of payment periods

■ calculation of interest to an accuracy of one day
■ calculation of time-based wages.

Specifying Date and Time

In order to be able to work with the date and time functions, you must be familiar with the method of specifying and editing date and time data. Attention should be given to several formal rules.

The date can be specified in the following way:

```
@DATE(year,month,day)
```

In this, the format for the year, month and day is YY,MM,DD.

Go to a random cell in the worksheet, for instance A1. Enter here the date 06/10/92. Thus:

```
@DATE(92,10,06)
```

After confirmation, the following screen will appear:

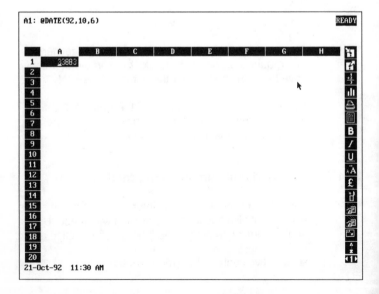

When a date is entered, Lotus 1-2-3 checks the plausibility of the specification. If this is adjudged to be reasonable, the date is shown as serial number on the screen. In this example, that is 33883. In Lotus 1-2-3, dates are displayed as serial integers between 1 and 73,050. 1 corresponds to January 1st 1900, 73,050 corresponds to 31st December 2099.

Cells containing a number like this can be formatted and converted to a date format via the Range Format Date submenu. The following figure shows the different possibilities:

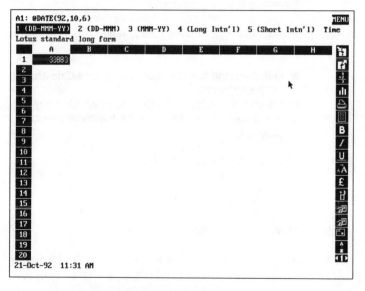

If you have chosen a certain option and have confirmed it using Enter, the date will be displayed in the selected form, if the column is wide enough to do this. There are also four different time formats.

It is also possible to display the current time. The function @NOW performs this. This function displays the serial number for the current date and time in the active cell.

Try this function out in cell A3. When you have entered
@NOW and have confirmed this using Enter, the serial
number for the current date and time appears on the
screen. If no battery powered clock is integrated in your
computer, it is necessary to enter the correct date and
time yourself when starting up the computer otherwise
this function will not be correctly applied.

Using the following exercise, we shall deal with further
possibilities for the date and time functions.

Exercise 2-10: Reminders

In order to check whether outstanding debts are paid on
time, we shall create a worksheet which :

- calculates the due date from the invoice date and the
  fulfilment period;
- referring to the current date, shows whether a reminder should be sent because the fulfilment period has
  elapsed.

The result should appear as follows:

Survey of reminders

Current date: 21/10/92

Customer	Invoice date	Fulfilment period (in days)	Due date	Reminder
Bob Fellini	12/07/92	75	25/09/92	Yes
Brad Jarmusch	28/06/92	90	26/09/92	Yes
Bonzo Frears	10/08/92	60	09/10/92	Yes
Beryl Campion	20/08/92	90	18/11/92	No
Biffo Scorcese	22/08/92	45	06/10/92	Yes
Billy Wenders	27/09/92	75	11/12/92	No

Notes:

■ Set the global column width to 14.
■ First enter the text data.
■ Then the independent values can be entered in column C (Fulfilment period).
■ Then enter the current date in B3 and the invoice dates in B9..B14.
■ Format the invoice dates in the desired display.
■ Calculate the due dates in column D.
■ A text must be entered in column E (Yes or No). This determines whether a reminder should be sent or not.
■ Save the worksheet under the name REMINDER.

We shall apply the input mentioned above and the format of date specification once more. Subsequently, we shall examine how this information can be used in calculations.

The solution to the problem can be divided into the following stages:

All text data must be entered at the appropriate positions: the title of the survey, the columns and the names of the customers. All text must be aligned properly.

The number values must be entered in column C. This deals with the fulfilment period in days.

The date input is entered using the function @DATE (year,month,day). This applies to the current date and also to the invoice dates. We shall use the @DATE function here for the current date for reasons of overview and uniformity. In practice, the @NOW function is probably preferable in order to apply the current date each time the worksheet is activated.

Using the Range Format Date submenu, the invoice dates can be displayed in column B in the desired format. Select option 4 (Long Int.'l).

As mentioned, Lotus 1-2-3 saves the date and time in-

ternally as decimal numbers. This enables the execution of mathematical operations using date and time
fields, or use of date or time in a formula. In order to calculate the appropriate due dates for the individual in-
voices, you must add the corresponding fulfilment period to the invoice date. Accordingly, the following
formula is created for field D9, which can then be copied
downwards:

```
+B9+C9
```

When the result cells have been formatted in the proper
way, the due date will be accurately shown in column D.

Whether or not a reminder should be sent is determined
by comparing the calculated due date to the current
date as specified in cell B4. The @IF function produces
the answer.

Thus, in field E9 the following formula should be entered:

```
@IF(D9<$B$3,"Yes","No")
```

And this formula can also be copied downwards.

Save this worksheet under the name REMINDER using
the command File Save.

If you have followed the above instructions precisely,
the worksheet should look like this:

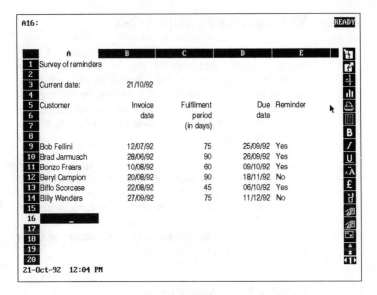

There are various functions for date and time in Lotus 1-2-3. We have now learned one of them. Using the Help screen or by consulting your manual, you can become familiar with the other date and time functions which Lotus 1-2-3 provides.

2.11.4 Summary of section 2.11

■ Using logical functions it is possible to create complex applications in Lotus 1-2-3. The @IF function in particular has special significance. This can also be used in conjunction with other functions and makes it possible to apply multiple claim hypotheses.

■ The financial mathematical functions in Lotus 1-2-3 provide extensive calculation possibilities for various applications in financial and economic areas.

■ Using date and time functions, worksheets can be made for debit administration, for instance.

2.12   Windows in Lotus 1-2-3

A feature of modern software is the possibility of splitting the screen into several parts, in effect to create more screens, in which work can be carried out independently. This so-called *window technique* offers great benefits in practice. In the case of spreadsheets, we can outline two substantial advantages of applying the window technique:

Division of the screen into separate windows benefits the **overview when working with large worksheets**. For instance, figures from different periods can be placed next to each other allowing quick comparison.

Using the window technique, it is much **easier** to **copy** parts of a worksheet to another table.

Exercise 2-11: Window technique

Load the TURNOVR3 file and with the help of the following exercise you will become acquainted with the possibilities of the window technique:

- activating a vertical window
- activating a horizontal window
- moving in windows
- deleting windows.

The command used to split the screen into windows can be found in the Worksheet Window submenu. The options in this menu have the following significance:

Horizontal	Splits the screen horizontally at the current row.
Vertical	Splits the screen vertically at the current column.
Sync	If the screen in one window is scrolled, the rows and columns in the other windows scroll as well.
Unsync	Scrolls windows independently.

Clear   Returns to full-screen display.

Using the cell pointer, go to column D in the file which
you have just loaded, TURNOVR3. Choose the Worksheet Window submenu and select the Vertical option.
After confirmation using Enter, the screen will be parti-
tioned into two columns as shown below.

C1:						READY
	A	**B**	**C**	**D**	**E**	**F**
1		Estimated		**1**	Real		Differ
2		Turnover x	Share in %	**2**	Turnover x	Share in %	Est.−R
3	Month	£1000		**3**	£1000		£
4				**4**			
5	January	150	4.2	**5**	132	3.9	
6	February	212	6.0	**6**	260	7.6	
7	March	222	6.2	**7**	322	9.4	
8	April	318	8.9	**8**	312	9.2	
9	May	344	9.7	**9**	322	9.4	
10	June	551	15.5	**10**	457	13.4	
11	July	180	5.1	**11**	234	6.9	
12	August	166	4.7	**12**	239	7.0	
13	September	300	8.4	**13**	234	6.9	
14	October	345	9.7	**14**	317	9.3	
15	November	433	12.2	**15**	345	10.1	
16	December	335	9.4	**16**	234	6.9	
17	---			**17**	---		
18	Total	3556		**18**	3408		
19	Maximum	551		**19**	457		
20	Minimum	150		**20**	132		

21-Oct-92   12:08 PM

The new window begins at column D. The cell pointer is
located in the original window. Horizontal windows can
be created in a similar manner. The function key F6 enables you to switch between the different windows.

The original situation is restored easily by selecting the
Clear option from the same submenu. The division into
windows is then undone.

2.13   Linking worksheets

A good spreadsheet program makes it possible to link
worksheets to one another. This considerably speeds

up working with electronic worksheets and increases the accuracy of the results.

There are various possibilities of addressing results from other worksheets. These results do not have to be entered separately - they can be adopted automatically.

Using the following exercise, we shall illustrate how data can be adopted from another worksheet to be further edited.

Exercise 2-12: Integration of worksheets

In the following worksheet, there are data which have to be adopted by another worksheet to be further edited. Save this worksheet under the name COSTS.

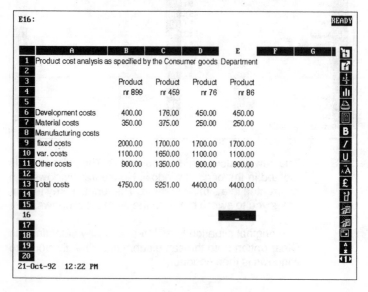

Then create the following worksheet and save it under the file name COSTEFF.

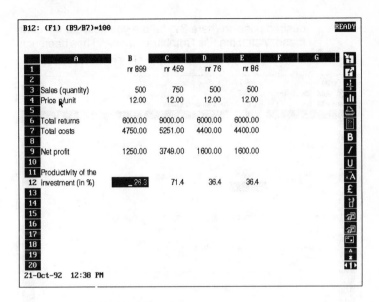

Now remove the values for the total costs. These values should then be adopted from the above worksheet COSTS.WK1.

We shall now create the first worksheet. This will serve as source worksheet. The total costs which are calculated here are to be used in other worksheets. To make this possible, the range containing the results must be given a name, for example, TOT_COSTS. Go with the cell pointer to field B12 and select the Range Name Create command. Specify the name TOT_COSTS and the range B12..E12. Then save the worksheet under the name COSTS.

Subsequently, create the worksheet COSTEFF.WK1 and delete the data from the row containing the total costs using the Range Erase command. In order to link both worksheets, we shall use the File Combine command. Using this, an entire worksheet or a part of it can be transported to an active worksheet. The entry then takes place at the current position of the cell pointer. For this reason, it is useful to place the cell pointer at the

desired position (here B7) before you activate the command. When the File Combine command has been activated, the following screen will appear:

```
B7: (F2)                                                          MENU
Copy  Add   Subtract
Copy data from a file on disk to the worksheet
```

	A	B	C	D	E	F	G
1		nr 899	nr 459	nr 76	nr 86		
2							
3	Sales (quantity)	500	750	500	500		
4	Price p/unit	12.00	12.00	12.00	12.00		
5							
6	Total returns	6000.00	9000.00	6000.00	6000.00		
7	Total costs						
8							
9							
10	Net profit	6000.00	9000.00	6000.00	6000.00		
11							
12	Productivity of the						
13	investment (in %)	26.3	71.4	36.4	36.4		
14							
15							
16							
17							
18							
19							
20							

```
21-Oct-92   12:33 PM
```

The figure shows that there are three options in the
menu to combine data from another file with the current
worksheet:

Copy   Copies the contents of the cell to the current
             worksheet.

Add   Adds the values of the cell contents to the
             values in the current worksheet. This can be
             useful, for instance, if various monthly work-
             sheets have to be added to a quarterly or
             annual worksheet.

Subtract Subtracts the cell contents from the values
             in the cells in the current worksheet.

For our example, we shall select the Copy option. The
choice is then offered between the Entire-File and

Named/Specified-Range options. We shall choose the second option, since we only wish to copy a part and not the entire file. A name has to be specified for this range, TOT_COSTS in this case, and then the name of the combined file. When the command has been confirmed, the selected data should be automatically copied to the current worksheet.

This procedure is as follows:

■ Using the cursor keys, go to the first cell of the range which is to be copied.
■ Activate the File Combine submenu using /FC.
■ Then choose in succession the options Copy and Named/Specified-Range.
■ Specify a name for the range and enter the name of the file.
■ Confirm the command using Enter.

The required data will subsequently appear in row 7. In this way, updating can be easily implemented if alterations take place in the source worksheet.

You will have noticed that this method only works if the total costs in COSTS.WK1 are **not** the result of formulas, but have been entered manually. Another method of linking worksheets to which this condition does not apply is the so-called **linking formula method**. This method works as follows: If you enter +<<COSTS.WK1>>B13 in cell B7 of COSTEFF.WK1 and copy this formula to C7..E7, you will see that the total costs are adopted from COSTS.WK1. If you change the data in COSTS.WK1, the values in COSTEFF.WK1 will also change.

```
B7: (F2) +<<COSTS.WK1>>B13                                            READY
```

	A	B	C	D	E	F	G
1		nr 899	nr 459	nr 76	nr 86		
2							
3	Sales (quantity)	500	750	500	500		
4	Price p/unit	12.00	12.00	12.00	12.00		
5							
6	Total returns	6000.00	9000.00	6000.00	6000.00		
7	Tota costs	4750.00	5251.00	4400.00	4400.00		
8							
9	Net profit	1250.00	3749.00	1600.00	1600.00		
10							
11	Productivity of the						
12	investment (in %)	26.3	71.4	36.4	36.4		
13							
14							
15							
16							
17							
18							
19							
20							

```
21-Oct-92  01:10 PM
```

2.13.1   Summary of section 2.13

■ Using the File Combine command, different worksheets can be linked to each other. The possible options here are: Copying, Adding and Subtracting data
from a source file to the current worksheet.

2.14   Macros in Lotus 1-2-3

It frequently occurs that certain procedures in a worksheet have to repeated a number of times. In order to
avoid having to go through the same manoeuvres time
and again, Lotus 1-2-3 provides the possibility of defining macros. We shall discuss the usage of macros
below, using the basic functions as the point of departure. We wish, however, to emphasize that macros can
also be applied in complex situations. Examples:

Interactive macros

It is possible to program a dialogue with the user by employing the question mark (?) when writing the program.

Self-starting macros

Each time a worksheet is loaded, Lotus 1-2-3 checks whether there is a macro present which should be automatically started up. This could be, for instance, an advice macro for writing reminders.

Macros with menus

It is possible to define commands in macros and, in this way, compose your own menus.

Extensive discussion about advanced macro commands lies outside the scope of this book. For more information consult the manual.

In principle, a macro is constructed in three stages:

- conceptualizing and entering
- assigning a name
- activating.

Referring to the following exercise, we shall deal with the structure and use of macros, with the basic functions as point of departure.

Exercise 2-13: Constructing and using macros

The transport of a range from one worksheet to another, as in the previous exercise, can be automatically executed if this concerns a frequently recurring procedure.

Write a macro for this in a suitable range.

Assign the shortcut key combination \K to this macro.

Subsequently save the worksheet COSTEFF under the name COSTEFF1 and use the macro.

2.14.1   Conceptualizing and entering the macro

When it is clear for which activity a macro is required, a plan of action has to be made. It is advisable to first test all the keystrokes to observe their effects and to note these carefully. In this example, you can make use of the step-by-step procedure as used in the previous example.

In the list of macro keys shown below, you can see the required keys and their corresponding significance for constructing a macro:

macro key	significance
~	Enter
{DOWN} or {D}	cursor downwards
{UP} or {U}	cursor upwards
{LEFT} or {L}	cursor leftwards
{RIGHT} or {R}	cursor rightwards
{HOME}	Home
{END}	End
{PGUP}	PgUp
{PGDN}	PgDn
{HELP}	HELP (F1)
{EDIT}	EDIT (F2)
{NAME}	NAME (F3)
{ABS}	ABS (F4)
{GOTO}	GOTO (F5)
{WINDOW}	WINDOW (F6)
{QUERY}	QUERY (F7)
{TABLE}	TABLE (F8)
{CALC}	CALC (F9)
{GRAPH}	GRAPH (F10)
{ESCAPE} or {ESC}	Esc
{BACKSPACE} or {BS}	Backspace

{DELETE} or {DEL}	Del
{BREAK}	Ctrl-Break
{INSERT} or {INS}	Ins
{BIGLEFT}	Ctrl-cursor leftwards or Shift-Tab
{BIGRIGHT}	Ctrl-cursor rightwards or Tab
/, < or {MENU}	slash (/) or smaller than sign (<)
{APP1}	APP1 (Alt-F7)
{APP2}	APP2 (Alt-F8)
{APP3}	APP3 (Alt-F9)
{APP4}	APP4 (Alt-F10)

Notes:

■ The names of the macro keys can be entered using both small and capital letters.
■ The last four commands (APP1 to APP4) activate add-ins directly. There is more information about this in section 5.3.

The macro in our example is as follows:

```
{GOTO}B7~/FCCNTOT_COSTS~COSTS.WK1~
```

The example illustrates that a macro may contain both special macro keys (between braces) and normal characters from the keyboard.

Now load the worksheet COSTEFF. First, remove the range B7..E7 from the worksheet. To construct the macro, an empty range must be found to prevent data which may be present influencing the macro. Go to cell B20 for example.

Now enter the above macro. The macro should be entered in the form of a label. Accordingly, an alignment character (an apostrophe) should be placed if the macro begins with a command, a number or a formula. The screen should appear as follows:

```
B20: '{goto}b7~/fccntot_costs~costs.wk1~                              READY
```

	A	B	C	D	E	F	G	
1		nr 899	nr 459	nr 76	nr 86			
2								
3	Sales (quantity)	500	750	500	500			
4	Price p/unit	12.00	12.00	12.00	12.00			
5								
6	Total returns	6000.00	9000.00	6000.00	6000.00			
7	Total costs							
8								
9	Net profit	6000.00	9000.00	6000.00	6000.00			
10								
11	Productivity of the							
12	investment (in %)	ERR	ERR	ERR	ERR			
13								
14								
15								
16								
17								
18								
19								
20		{goto}b7~ fccntot_costs~ costs.wk1 ~						

```
21-Oct-92   02:07 PM
```

When entering a macro, the following formal rules should be kept in mind:

■ The macro should be placed in one particular column.
■ A macro command may contain a maximum of 240 characters per cell.
■ Longer macros are continued on the next line.
■ In order to prevent data and macro commands being confused, the cell under the entered macro instructions should be left empty.

2.14.2   Assigning a name to the macro

Before a macro can be implemented, a name must be assigned to it using the Range Name Create command. There you should specify a name as a range name, which means that a macro name can only consist of a backslash followed by one of the letters of the alphabet, thus: \A to \Z.

Accordingly, the procedure when assigning a name to a macro is as follows:

- Using the cursor keys, go to the first cell.
- Activate the Range Name Create submenu using /RNC.
- Assign a name to the macro, for example, \K.
- Press Enter twice to execute the command and confirm the range.

In order to confirm the command and the specified range it is sufficient to activate only the starting position or the first cell of the total macro. Thus, it is not necessary to specify the whole range.

Now that the macro has been allocated a name, it can be used in conjunction with the worksheet. For later use, it is absolutely necessary to save the worksheet using File Save. Give the worksheet the name COSTEFF1.

2.14.3   Running a macro

When implementing a macro, use is made of a macro letter which has been allocated beforehand. This is \K in the example in question. By pressing this key along with the Alt key, the values in the source worksheet COSTS are automatically transported to the worksheet COSTEFF1. The result is as follows:

```
B7: (F2) 4750                                                    READY

           A         B        C        D        E        F       G
  1                 nr 899   nr 459   nr 76    nr 86
  2
  3  Sales (quantity)  500     750      500      500
  4  Price p/unit     12.00   12.00    12.00    12.00
  5
  6  Total returns   6000.00  9000.00  6000.00  6000.00
  7  Total costs     4750.00  5251.00  4400.00  4400.00
  8
  9  Net profit      1250.00  3749.00  1600.00  1600.00
 10
 11  Productivity of the
 12  investment (in %)  26.3   71.4     36.4     36.4
 13
 14
 15
 16
 17
 18
 19
 20                  {goto}b7~/fccntot_costs~costs.wk1 ~
21-Oct-92  02:08 PM
```

Notes:

- A macro is implemented by pressing the Alt key together with the allocated letter. The backslash is only used when the name is being assigned.
- A macro can be interrupted by pressing Break.
- A macro can be altered later, if required, in the same way as labels.
- A long macro can be tested out step-by-step using the STEP function which is activated by pressing Alt-F2. Afterwards, you activate the macro as you normally would.

2.14.4   Summary of section 2.14

- Use of macros can considerably alleviate working with Lotus 1-2-3 if certain procedures have to be repeated. Common applications for macros are: automating series of commands which are frequently used, implementing a procedure which repeats itself and the construction of a personal worksheet.

- Before beginning a macro, you must formulate exactly what you expect from the macro. In addition, a macro which has been constructed must be carefully tested.
- Menu instructions, special keys and random cell data may be included in a macro.
- You assign a name to a macro in the Range Name Create submenu by typing a backslash followed by a letter, for example, \K.
- The macro is activated by pressing the Alt key simultaneously with the assigned letter.

Exercises

(1)   Development of the apprenticeship system

A large industrial company is interested in developing its apprenticeship system further with respect to the choice of pupils. The exercise consists of visualizing this development and carrying out various calculations. The result should be the following worksheet:

```
A17: [W12]                                                         READY

         A          B       C       D       E       F       G    H
 1  Job             1987    1988    1989    1990    Total
 2  ---------------------------------------------------------
 3  Comm.-adm.      123     143     154     139     559
 4  assistant
 5  Administr.      87      76      128     98      389
 6  assistant
 7  Comm.-sales     145     132     122     135     534
 8  assistant
 9  Mechanic        234     254     266     270     1024
10  Lab.tech.       453     421     432     409     1715
11  Craftsman       211     234     267     344     1056
12  ---------------------------------------------------------
13  Total           1253    1260    1369    1395    5277
14  Average         208.8   210.0   228.2   232.5   879.5
15  Commercial
16  share           28.3    27.9    29.5    26.7    28.1
17
18
19
20
21-Oct-92  02:16 PM
```

The exercise is carried out in Lotus 1-2-3 in the following stages:

(a)   entering text and number values
(b)   constructing formulas for the calculation of the totals and averages and for the share of commercial staff
(c)   formatting the average values and share with one place behind the decimal point
(d)   printing the worksheet in its entirety, and with only the formulas
(e)   saving the worksheet under the name AP-PRENT.

(2)   **Calculating an invoice sum**

Create the following worksheet using formulas based on fixed data concerning 'Quantity' and 'Price per unit'. These enable you to calculate the gross sum. If more than 100 articles are ordered a discount of 15% is given.

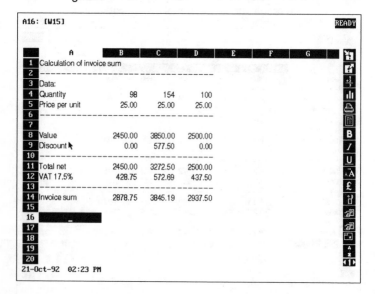

	A	B	C	D	E	F	G
1	Calculation of invoice sum						
2	----						
3	Data:						
4	Quantity	98	154	100			
5	Price per unit	25.00	25.00	25.00			
6	----						
7							
8	Value	2450.00	3850.00	2500.00			
9	Discount	0.00	577.50	0.00			
10	----						
11	Total net	2450.00	3272.50	2500.00			
12	VAT 17.5%	428.75	572.69	437.50			
13	----						
14	Invoice sum	2878.75	3845.19	2937.50			
15							
16							
17							
18							
19							
20							

A16: [W15]   READY

21-Oct-92   02:23 PM

Save the worksheet under the name INVOICE.

(3) Quotation comparison

A spreadsheet can provide valuable assistance when comparing quotations. A worksheet constructed for this purpose can look like this:

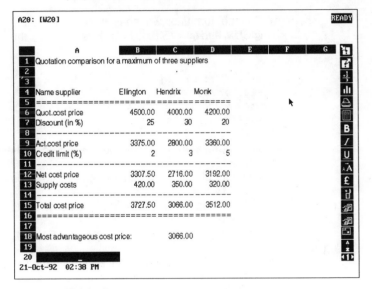

```
A20: [W20]                                                      READY

            A            B        C        D      E      F      G
 1  Quotation comparison for a maximum of three suppliers
 2
 3
 4  Name supplier      Ellington  Hendrix  Monk
 5  ==============================================
 6  Quot.cost price     4500.00  4000.00  4200.00
 7  Discount (in %)          25       30       20
 8  ---------------------------------------------
 9  Act.cost price      3375.00  2800.00  3360.00
10  Credit limit (%)          2        3        5
11  ---------------------------------------------
12  Net cost price      3307.50  2716.00  3192.00
13  Supply costs         420.00   350.00   320.00
14  ---------------------------------------------
15  Total cost price    3727.50  3066.00  3512.00
16  ==============================================
17
18  Most advantageous cost price:        3066.00
19
20
21-Oct-92  02:38 PM
```

The known values to be entered are:

- the official cost price
- the conditions, such as the quantity discount and credit limits
- the supply costs.

Save the worksheet under the name QUOTATN.

Procedures

(1) (a) The text data should be placed in the first column and in cell F1. Make the first column a little
wider in order to make meaningful, legible ab-
breviations (menu /WCS12). The numbers are
placed in columns B to E, in the rows 3 to 11.

(b) For the formulas we shall make use of the
@SUM and @AVE functions. This concerns the
following formulas:

```
B13:  @SUM(B3..B11)
B14:  @AVG(B3..B11)
B16:  @SUM(B3..B7)/B13*100
F3:   @SUM(B3..E3)
```

The formula in B13 can be copied to cells
C13..F13.
The formula in B14 can be copied to cells
C14..F14.
The formula in B16 can be copied to cells
C16..F16.
The formula in F3 can be copied to cell F4..F11.

(c) When you have activated cell B14 using the cell
pointer, you can specify the number of places
behind the decimal point (1 in this case) using
Range Format Fixed. Then specify range
B14..F16.

(d) The worksheet can be printed using Print
Printer. When you have specified the range, you
can transport the worksheet to the printer. The
formulas are printed via Print Printer Options
Other.

(e) Save the worksheet under the name APPRENT
using the File Save command.

(2)   When the text and number data are known, cal-
        culate the value of the goods in cell B8. Use the
        formula:

```
+B4*B5
```

This formula can subsequently be copied to
cells C8..D8.

The calculation of the discount depends upon
the quantity supplied, that is, upon whether this
figure is greater than 100. This gives rise to the
following formula:

```
@IF(B4>100,B8*0.15,0)
```

Copy this formula twice to the right.

The following formulas apply to the other cells to
which they can also be copied:

```
B11:  +B8-B9
B12:  +B11*0.175
B14:  +B11+B12
```

(3)   When all the known data have been entered, the
        formulas can be constructed. In order to calcu-
        late the actual cost price in row 9, we can use
        the following formula:

```
quot.cost price - (discount perc. *
cost price / 100)
```

This is:

```
+B6-(B7*B6/100)
```

This formula can be adopted in columns C and
D using the Copy command from the main
menu. The same applies to the formula which
calculates the net cost price.

The cost price is calculated by adding the supply costs (e.g. transport) to the net cost price.

Using a statistical function, the lowest cost price can be determined. Use the @MIN(range) function for this. The range is B15..D15 in this case.

3   Charts and diagrams

3.1   Survey of the graphic possibilities

Use of the PC with graphic applications is enormously on the increase. Keeping the diverse processing methods in mind, different sorts of graphic software can be distinguished:

- **Business graphics**. These deal with the display of numerical data in survey diagrams.
- **Drawing programs** (draw and paint software). Using these, it is possible to display procedures and links clearly.
- **Design and illustration programs**. These are applied in the creative design of different types of charts in technical and commercial fields.
- Software to support **image editing**. This deals chiefly with the import of existing drawings, photographs and video pictures.
- **Desktop publishing**. Using this software, it is possible to produce high quality proofs in which text and graphics can be combined.

Lotus 1-2-3 enables you to construct business graphics. The point of departure here is the orderly display of data and results in tables for planning and presentation. The objective of business graphics programs is to convert the numerical data into line, bar and pie charts. Business graphics are applied to the following areas of management and administration in particular:

(a)   management
  – graphically processing the most diverse data
  – presentation of results
(b)   finance and administration
  – internal company reports
  – comparison of estimated and real results
  – analysis of current developments
(c)   sales/marketing/advertising

  – analysis of sales development (comparison with estimated figures, preliminary forecasts)
  – diverse presentation
  – brochures
(d) production/material policy
  – calculation of relevant data
  – points of departure in production planning
  – display of technical data (measuring/test data)
(e) staff policy
  – analysis of personnel
  – assistance in staff planning

Various benefits are connected to the use of business graphics in the areas mentioned. For the decision-makers at management level in particular, they can provide welcome assistance in the execution of their work. Charts give a quicker and clearer survey of relevant data than lists and tables in the traditional presentation. Complex relationships are also easier to understand, important information is comprehended more quickly and is retained longer. Department managers and heads of sales, marketing and financial planning can gain advantage using these business graphics. This refers to both a better documentation of results and the possibility of formulating reports more rapidly and cheaply.

3.1.1   Summary of section 3.1

■ Lotus 1-2-3 can be used to create business graphics. This should not be confused with other modern graphic applications such as drawing, design, illustration and desktop publishing.
■ Business graphics deal with the conversion of numerical data into orderly diagrams.
■ Business graphics can be usefully applied in all sectors of a company: management, finance and administration, sales and marketing, and various other activities with an analytical nature.
■ Important advantages of using business graphics

are: better documentation of results, clear and simple representation of complex situations.

3.2 Types of charts and diagrams and their variants

The existing or specially entered data in an electronic worksheet are the point of departure for graphics in Lotus 1-2-3. In this, the numerical data in this worksheet can be converted into different types of charts and diagrams (Lotus 1-2-3 calls most of them 'graphs').

Each program which creates business graphics contains a certain number of variants. The following seven types are available in Lotus 1-2-3. The choice of type depends on the application:

chart type	description
Line diagram	Separate points are joined by a line: this is specially suited to display developments with the passage of time.
Bar chart	Bar charts make it possible to place different series of information next to one another. In addition to the display of time-oriented developments, these are very suited to the comparison of values in similar groups of data.
XY chart	This serves to clarify the relation between a unit X and a unit Y.
Stacked bar chart	Different series of data are displayed in a bar above one another.
Pie chart	This is especially suited to the display of parts of a whole.
HLCO chart	HLCO charts track fluctuations in data during a specific period of time, such as the high, low, closing and opening of stock prices.

Mixed chart   Mixed charts combine lines and bars
                     in the same graph.

The diverse charts can be supplemented with relevant
information and texts, such as:

■ headers and subtitles
■ suitable names for the axes
■ legends.

In addition, there are specific functions for giving various diagrams a certain layout, for example, with curves
and line patterns, colours and letter types.

3.2.1   Summary of section 3.2

■ Programs which create business graphics contain a
  number of graphic types. Lotus 1-2-3 provides the
  line diagram, the XY chart, the bar chart, the stacked
  bar chart, the pie chart, the HLCO chart and the
  mixed chart.
■ The type of diagram chosen depends upon the application.
■ In addition, there are various functions to embellish
  the diagrams: headers and titles, legends, curves etc.

3.3   Procedure when constructing a chart

We shall proceed as follows when constructing a chart
in Lotus 1-2-3:

■ A table containing values must be located in the
  worksheet.
■ We shall specify the chart: definition and parameters.
■ The chart will be displayed on the screen.
■ The chart will be saved.
■ The chart will be printed out.

We shall use the following exercise to become familiar with these manoeuvres.

Exercise 3-1: Creating a simple chart

In a company, the development of the returns over the last eight years should be presented in chart form. The values are as follows:

Year	Returns x £1 million
1985	120
1986	102
1987	105
1988	128
1989	137
1990	154
1991	156
1992	166

Create a line diagram which shows the development of these returns. Save the worksheet under the name SUCCESS1 and the diagram under the name DIAG-RAM1. Print the diagram on the printer.

3.3.1   Input of data for the diagram

To construct a diagram, the required data must be entered in a worksheet. The screen then appears as follows:

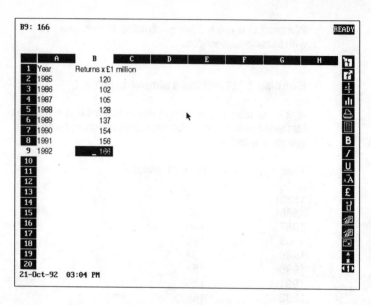

To create the diagram, you must now select Graph from the main menu (/G). The following options are available:

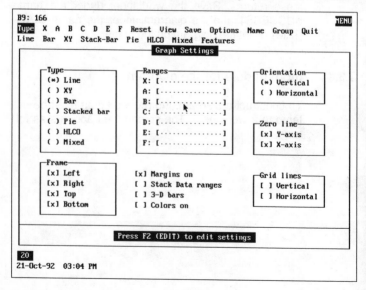

There are two different types of options:

Options which determine the graphic parameters:

■ Type determines the form of the chart or diagram.
■ X is for the input of X data.
■ A to F define the ranges to be included.
■ Reset restores the parameters to the default values.
■ Options provides options for titles, legends, colours etc.

Commands to implement Graphic operations:

■ View shows the current graph on the screen (preview function).
■ Save saves the current graph as a .PIC file to be used or printed out later.
■ Name names and manages different graphs in a worksheet.
■ Quit brings you back to the READY mode.

3.3.2   Specifying the parameters of a graph

In order to create a graph from particular values in a worksheet, you must specify certain parameters of the graph to conform to the required objectives. These concern:

■ determining the form of the graph
■ defining the data ranges
■ specific instructions for the layout of the graph (titles, axes texts and legends).

Specifying the type of graph

Firstly, the type of graph must be chosen. This should be the type which is most suitable for displaying the data. This occurs using the Type option, which provides the following possibilities:

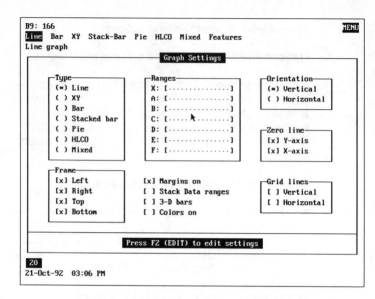

The figure shows seven types of graphs and diagrams in abbreviated form. Depending on the objectives and data, a selection should be made. Proceed as follows:

■ Select the Graph submenu and then the Type option using /GT.
■ Choose a certain type, in this case, the line diagram using L.

The line diagram is the default setting. We shall create a line diagram in our example, because this type of graph is well-suited to the display of changing numerical values with the passage of time. Thus, you do not need to change anything here.

Selecting the X range

In addition to the graph type, you must also, of course, specify the range from which the data should be extracted. Enter the appropriate ranges from the worksheet. There are seven letters available for the specification of ranges. The X range is specified here for line diagrams and (stack) bar charts. The program places the information contained in this range as labels at even distances along the horizontal axis of the chart or diagram. The letters A to F represent the so-called *data ranges*. This refers to normal ranges from the worksheet. These determine both the values to be displayed and the labels in the graph. Specify the range just as you would do in the worksheet:

- by specifying the cell addresses, or
- by activating the initial cell, anchoring it using the period key and then determining the end of the range using Enter, or
- by specifying range names.

As mentioned, we shall represent the development of the returns in a line diagram. The information which is to be used as labels under the X axis should be specified as the X range. In our case, that is the year list, 1985 to 1992. Proceed as follows to enter this:

- Activate the X range using X.
- Define the area A2..A9 in the worksheet.
- Confirm using Enter.

Before confirmation, the screen appears as follows:

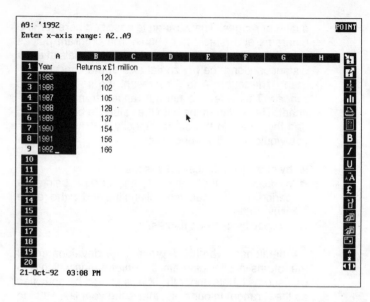

Thus, the range which is to be adopted is defined. When you press Enter, the program will return to the Graph menu.

Selecting the data range

You can specify the data range in the same way. In Lotus 1-2-3, a maximum of six data ranges is possible, A to F. In our example, we are dealing with only one data range. Accordingly, select the letter A by pressing the A key. Subsequently, using the cursor keys, or specifying directly, register the range B2..B9. If you specify the range using the cursor keys, the screen will appear as follows:

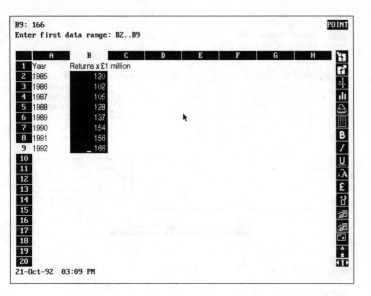

When you confirm this input using Enter, the most important data for the chart have been defined. You can see that the ranges you have defined are adopted in the Graph Settings menu.

Specifying titles for a graph

The graph can be given a title and the axes can display information to help clarify the chart. This information is registered using Graph Options Titles. When you have activated this submenu, the following menu will be displayed:

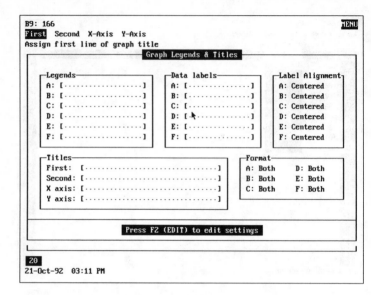

The options have the following significance:

option   significance

First   for the first title in the graph header

Second   for a second title, if required, above the
             graph

X-Axis   for information along the X axis. The text is
             centred under the axis.

Y-Axis   for information along the Y axis. The text is
             left of and parallel to the Y axis

Select the First option. This determines the main title of
the graph. In our example, that is 'Development of Returns'. The screen will then appear as follows:

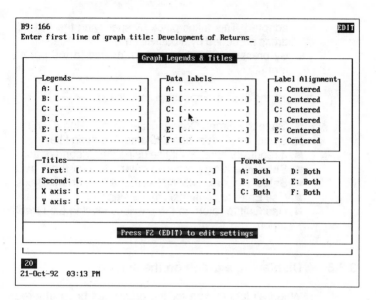

```
B9: 166                                                              EDIT
Enter first line of graph title: Development of Returns_

                    ┌─────── Graph Legends & Titles ───────┐

  ┌─Legends──────────────┐  ┌─Data labels────────┐  ┌─Label Alignment─┐
  A: [··················]    A: [··············]     A: Centered
  B: [··················]    B: [··············]     B: Centered
  C: [··················]    C: [··············]     C: Centered
  D: [··················]    D: [ ▴············]     D: Centered
  E: [··················]    E: [··············]     E: Centered
  F: [··················]    F: [··············]     F: Centered
  └──────────────────────┘  └────────────────────┘  └─────────────────┘

  ┌─Titles───────────────────────────────┐  ┌─Format────────────────┐
  First:  [·····························]     A: Both      D: Both
  Second: [·····························]     B: Both      E: Both
  X axis: [·····························]     C: Both      F: Both
  Y axis: [·····························]
  └───────────────────────────────────────┘ └───────────────────────┘

                 ┌ Press F2 (EDIT) to edit settings ┐

  L
  ┌──┐
  │20│
  └──┘
  21-Oct-92  03:13 PM
```

Confirm this using Enter. If necessary, you can also specify a second (sub)title, for example, 'between 1985 and 1992'. Both titles are displayed centred above the graph, the first title being larger than the second.

In addition to the title for the graph, other clarifications should be placed next to the axes. For this, we shall first deal with the X axis option where we shall specify the text 'Year'. We shall then do the same for the Y axis option where the text 'Returns in £m' should be placed. This text will be displayed left of and parallel to the Y axis.

Keep the following rules in mind when entering texts:

■ Titles in Lotus 1-2-3 may not contain more than 39 characters.
■ When choosing a subtitle, a title which is already displayed can be adopted using Enter. A title already in use can be removed using Esc and a new title can then be entered.
■ In all four options, the contents of a cell can also be

adopted. This takes place by specifying the cell address preceded by a backslash.

■ By pressing Quit the program moves to the parent menu.

Thus, the titles are specified as follows:

■ Go to the Graph Options Titles menu using /GOT.
■ Select the First option and enter the main title.
■ If required, enter a subtitle using the Second option.
■ Select the X axis option to enter a text for the X axis.
■ Select the Y axis option to enter a text for the Y axis.
■ Use Enter to confirm all these steps.
■ Use Quit to return to the previous level in the Graph menu.

3.3.3 Displaying a graph on the screen

When all information for the graph has been entered, you can display it on the screen by selecting the corresponding option, View, in the Graph menu. The following screen will appear:

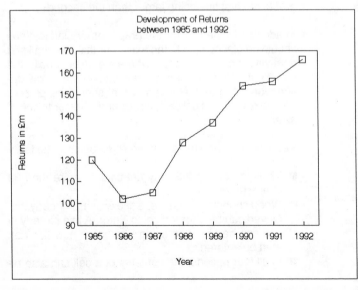

Instead of selecting View in the Graph menu, you can also press F10. This can be done at any time you wish, not only when you are in the Graph menu.

There are various methods of displaying charts and diagrams on the screen, depending on the monitor and the installed drivers:

Mixed mode. In this, graphs or texts and number series can be displayed simultaneously.

Switch mode. In this, only one type of window is displayed, either graphic or the table/text.

Double screen mode. If two monitors are connected, a display of texts (menu and parameters) and a display of graphs (for the display of the actual chart) can be given in the graphic window.

The program returns to the menu when you press a random key.

It is possible to change a chosen type of graph using Graph Type in which another option can be selected. In addition, the data in the worksheet can also be altered later. Alteration of specified graphic or range parameters takes place in the Graph Reset menu. This menu provides the following options (page 156).

The options have the following significance:

Graph	All the current parameters are removed.
X to F	If one of these letters is chosen the data from the corresponding range are suppressed.
Ranges	Removes the settings for all data ranges with data labels if present.
Options	All settings in Graph Options are removed.
Quit	Use Quit to return to the Graph menu.

To carry out our example, no changes need to be made.

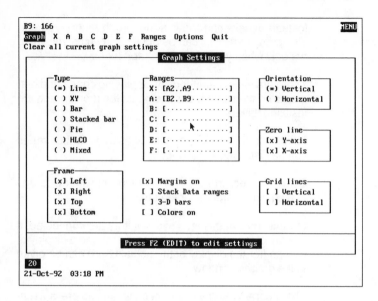

3.3.4   Saving a chart

Lotus 1-2-3 saves a chart when the Save command from the Graph menu is activated. You will be asked to enter a name for the file.

If you accept the default drive and directory, you only have to specify a file name, in this case GRAPH1. The program will automatically assign the extension .PIC. If the file GRAPH1.PIC has been saved in this way, it can now be printed using the print program PrintGraph which is supplied along with the package, or using another compatible program.

It may also be useful to first save the graph using Graph Name Create. It is then possible to make more charts from the same worksheet. We shall return to this topic later.

If you wish to use the worksheet later, you must save it separately using File Save. Save our example worksheet under the name SUCCESS1.

3.3.5   Printing a chart

In Lotus 1-2-3, a chart is printed using the PrintGraph program which is supplied with the package. Thus, it is not possible to print the chart directly - a separate graphic file of the chart must be created first. Subsequently, quit 1-2-3 and load the PrintGraph program which can then print the chart on a printer or plotter.

The procedure is as follows:

- Save the chart
- Save the worksheet
- Quit 1-2-3
- Start up PrintGraph
- Specify the required parameters
- Select the chart
- Print the chart.

In the PrintGraph program, it is not possible to make alterations to the chart. That can only be done in Lotus 1-2-3.

Starting up PrintGraph

To activate the PrintGraph program from the DOS command line, type 'pgraph'. It is also possible to activate the program from the Access menu. When the program has been activated, the following screen with parameters will appear:

```
Copyright 1986, 1991, 1992 Lotus Development Corp.  All Rights Reserved.  MENU

Select graphs to print or preview
Image-Select  Settings  Go  Align  Page  Exit

    GRAPHS     IMAGE SETTINGS                       HARDWARE SETTINGS
    TO PRINT   Size                Range colors       Graphs directory
               Top        1.00     X                    C:\123R24
               Left       1.90     A                  Fonts directory
               Width     16.51     B                    C:\123R24
               Height    11.91     C                  Interface
               Rotation   .000     D                    Parallel 1
                                   E                  Printer
               Font                F
               1  BLOCK1                              Paper size
               2  BLOCK1                                Width     21.59
                                                        Length    27.94

                                                      ACTION SETTINGS
                                                      Pause  No   Eject  No
```

In the menu there are six basic commands with the following significance:

command	significance
Image-Select	Graphic files, equipped with the extension .PIC, can be selected to be printed.
Settings	Specify and alter the graphic parameters such as the size of the chart, font and hardware used.
Go	Start printing.
Align	Inform PrintGraph that you have positioned the paper at the top of a page.
Page	The paper is advanced to the top of the next page.
Exit	Closes PrintGraph.

Print settings

Before beginning with printing, the correct settings for the corresponding chart should be chosen. This concerns the layout, the font, the colours and the hardware configuration. Check whether the proper parameters have been specified.

After selecting the Settings option the following screen will appear:

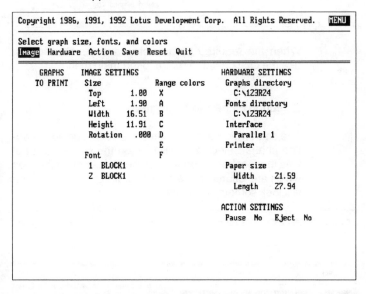

The options Image, Hardware, Action, Save, Reset and Quit appear on the Control Panel. Select the Hardware option and specify the appropriate parameters. Use the C:\123R24 directory for the charts and do the same for the fonts. Then choose the type of printer. Keep in mind that this printer must have been specified during installation. This should produce a screen similar to this:

```
Copyright 1986, 1991, 1992 Lotus Development Corp.  All Rights Reserved.  POINT

Select graphics printer or plotter


   Printer or Plotter name and Resolution
   --------------------------------------------  Space bar marks or unmarks selection
   HP LaserJet IIP and IIP+  150 DPI            ENTER selects marked device
   HP LaserJet IIP and IIP+  300 DPI            ESC exits, ignoring changes
                                                HOME moves to beginning of list
                                                END moves to end of list
                                                ↑ and ↓ move highlight
                                                  List will scroll if highlight
                                                  moved beyond top or bottom
```

When the required parameters have been specified,
use the Quit option to return to the main menu.

Selecting a chart to be printed

The chart which is to be printed is selected using the option Image-Select. You will see, on the screen, a list of
files in alphabetical order with the names of all the files
which are located in the specified directory. The screen
will look something like this:

```
Copyright 1986, 1991, 1992 Lotus Development Corp.  All Rights Reserved.  POINT

Select graphs to print


   GRAPH FILE  DATE      TIME    SIZE
   --------------------------------------  Space bar marks or unmarks selection
   BILLY     10-21-92  14:34    2410       ENTER selects marked graphs
   BINKER    10-21-92  15:44     439       ESC exits, ignoring changes
   GRAPH1    10-21-92  15:20     950       HOME moves to beginning of list
   HILL      10-21-92  15:44     877       END moves to end of list
                                           ↑ and ↓ move highlight
                                             List will scroll if highlight
                                             moved beyond top or bottom
                                           GRAPH (F10) previews marked graph
```

The file list shows the time when the file was created
and the amount of bytes occupied by the file.

Selecting a file to be printed takes place as follows. Using the cursor, go to the file which is to be printed and press the spacebar. The file is marked with a number sign (#). The marking is switched off again by repeating the procedure.

Using the GRAPH key (F10), marked files can be shown on the screen to be checked before printing. To carry out the current exercise, mark the file GRAPH1 and check the chart using F10. The appropriate chart should appear on the screen. Confirm the chart using Enter. The program then returns to the main menu.

Thus, the entire procedure is as follows:

■ Select the Image-Select option using I.
■ Use the cursor keys to go to the desired file.
■ Mark the file with a number sign by pressing the spacebar.
■ Confirm using Enter. The program returns to the main menu.

The print command

When the required chart has been summoned using Image-Select and the correct parameters have been set, the paper should be placed in the proper position. This is done using the Align option. Subsequently, you can give the Go command.

It is also possible to simultaneously activate various charts to be printed. Printing will begin immediately if all parameters have been properly specified. It is then not necessary to confirm the print command once more.

Messages appear on the Control Panel during printing, for example, WAIT. You can discontinue printing using the Break key. When all print instructions have been carried out, the program returns to the main menu.

Quitting PrintGraph

The program can be closed using the Exit option. Before you can definitely leave the program, you will be asked whether you really wish to end working with Print-Graph. If you have activated the program from the Access menu, you will return to it by selecting Yes. Otherwise Yes will return you to DOS.

3.3.6   Summary of section 3.3

■ The data required to make a chart must be located in a worksheet or must be entered there.

■ To make a business graph in Lotus 1-2-3, select the Graph option. The relevant data can be specified there.

■ There are seven different types of chart and diagram in Lotus 1-2-3: Line diagram, Bar chart, Stacked bar chart, XY chart, Pie chart, HLCO (high, low, closing, opening) and Mixed. The most suitable diagram to express the relevant data can be chosen under Type.

■ The range data determine the values when creating a chart.

■ Titles for the chart and for the axes can be specified in the menu Graph Options Titles.

■ Graphs are saved using the menu Graph Save. The program assigns the extension .PIC to the file name specified by the user.

■ Charts are printed using the separate print program PrintGraph.

3.4   Line diagram with various ranges

The line diagram is especially suited to the display of time-oriented data. Comparison of different aspects, such as the development of returns and overheads can be readily made. We shall illustrate this using the following example:

Exercise 3-2: Create a line diagram using various ranges

In the example in exercise 3-1, the costs showed the following development:

Year	Costs x £1 million
1985	98
1986	110
1987	102
1988	103
1989	113
1990	125
1991	130
1992	137

Enter the costs in the Lotus table SUCCESS1.WK1 and then place the returns and the costs opposite each other in a line diagram. Save the result under the name GRAPH2. Save the worksheet under the name SUC-CESS2.WK1.

3.4.1   Creating and adopting different ranges

If we wish to compare the returns and the costs, we must first enter the costs in the SUCCESS1 file. Load the file using File Retrieve and enter the cost data in column D. The worksheet will appear as follows:

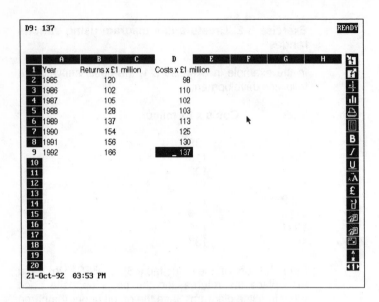

Then activate the Graph menu to specify the range B.
The marking will look like this:

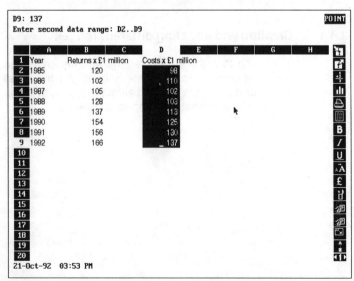

Confirm this using Enter and the second range is activated. Costs and returns can be simultaneously displayed in a graph, which enables comparison between
both units.

The first title of the chart must now be changed to
'Costs/Returns Development'. This takes place in the
usual way via Graph Options Titles. Select the First option. The title of the Y axis should also be altered to 'In
£m'. Then quit the menu and return to the Graph menu.

Subsequently check the result using the View option.
The screen should appear as follows:

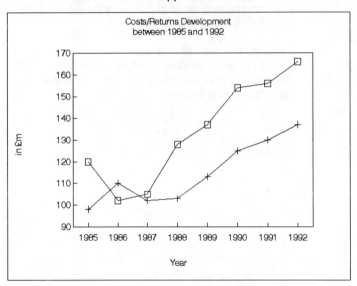

3.4.2   Adding a legend

Because two ranges are now being shown, in the form
of two lines, it is advisable to add a legend for better
orientation. This clarifies the significance of the two
lines in the graph, i.e. which line displays the returns
figures and which line the costs. In the case of bar

charts and stacked bar charts, a legend should contain an explanation of the colours or the curves in use.

When specifying a legend, it is very useful if a suitable text has already been included in the worksheet, for example, as a title of a column. Then the specification of the cell address is sufficient.

The procedure is thus as follows:

■ Activate the Graph Options menu using /GO.
■ Select the Legend option.
■ For the first range at A, specify the legend 'Returns'.
■ For the second range at B, specify the legend 'Costs'.
■ Use Quit to return to the main menu.

If you specify the cell address instead of a name, you should place a backslash in front of the address. The cell address may also be a range name. The line diagram appears as follows:

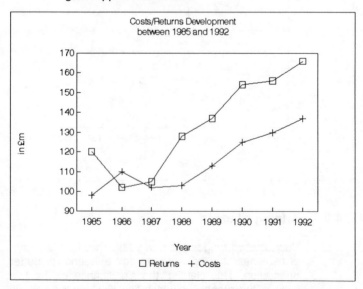

As you will observe, the legend is automatically placed

under the X axis. The symbol corresponds to the symbol used on the line.

3.4.3 Changing the line format

It is possible to format the lines in a certain way in line diagrams and XY charts. This takes place using Graph Options Format. Here you can determine whether the format should apply to the entire chart or only to certain ranges.

If you select the Graph option, the following screen will appear:

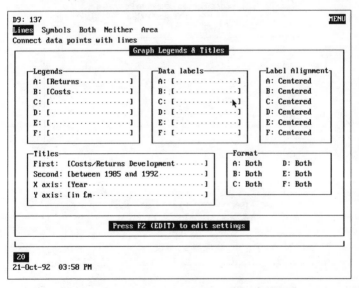

The options have the following significance:

Lines   The data points are connected by lines. There are no symbols on the lines.

Symbols   The data points are displayed as symbols. There is a separate symbol for each of the six ranges.

Both   Both lines and symbols are displayed. This
            is the default setting.

Neither   No values are displayed initially. That is
            done using the Data Labels function. Thus,
            only the labels make the data points visible.

Area   The area under the lines is filled in.

Try out the Symbols option and display the chart on the
screen using View:

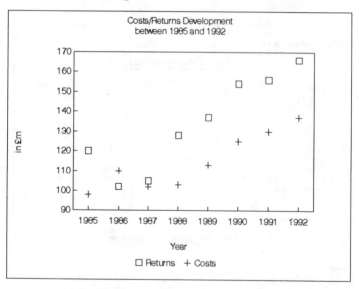

Subsequently, return to the Graph Options Format
Graph menu and restore the default setting using Both.
The Quit option will return you to the Graph Options
menu.

3.4.4 Adding gridlines

In order to connect certain values to one another more quickly when viewing a chart, it can be very useful to add gridlines to the chart. This is possible using Graph Options Grid. Here, the following options are available:

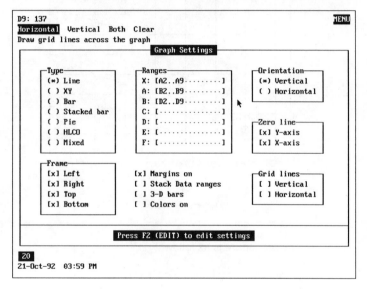

These options have the following significance:

option | **significance**

Horizontal   Draws horizontal gridlines in the chart, beginning at the left-hand side.

Vertical   Draws vertical gridlines in the chart, beginning at the bottom.

Both   Draws horizontal and vertical gridlines in the chart.

Clear   No gridlines in the chart. Any lines present will be removed.

If you select Both, View (or F10) will display the following screen:

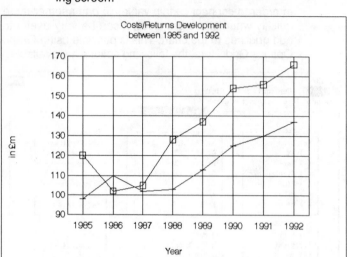

The procedure is as follows:

- Activate Graph Options Grid using /GOG.
- Select the required option, for example, Both using B.

It is also possible to equip (stack) bar charts and XY charts with gridlines. This option will not work with pie charts. Parameters which have been set here will be ignored.

3.4.5   Using Data Labels

Another method of clarification of the lines is to supply the individual points in the chart with the corresponding values. First remove the gridlines added in the previous section. Then go to the Graph Options Data-Labels menu. Here you must specify the range again: B2..B9 for A and C2..C9 for B.

In both cases, select the display option Below. The result should correspond to the figure below:

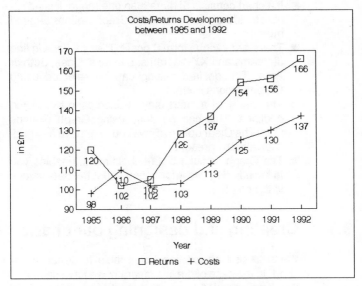

Costs/Returns Development
between 1985 and 1992

As you will observe, the program places the data labels in the line diagram exactly under the data points. As you will also observe, this may have the disadvantage of producing a rather 'crowded' diagram.

The procedure of placing data labels is thus as follows:

- Go to Graph Options Data-Labels.
- Specify the corresponding data ranges in the worksheet.
- Confirm the values by pressing Enter.
- Select a display form for the labels, in this case Below using B.

Return to the Graph menu using Quit. Finally, save the worksheet under the name SUCCESS2 and the chart under the name GRAPH2.

3.4.6   Summary of section 3.4

■ If a chart consists of more than one range, it is advisable to add a legend using the Graph Options Legend menu.

■ There are various format possibilities for lines in line diagrams and XY diagrams: Symbols, Lines, Both or Area. The desired setting can be selected using Graph Options Format.

■ The clarity of a chart may be increased by adding gridlines. This can be done using Graph Options Grid. The Clear option allows you to remove any gridlines already present.

■ The Graph Options Data-Labels menu enables you to include detailed information about the data values in the chart.

3.5   Creating and designing bar charts

We shall use an existing Lotus table to create a bar chart. In the case of the line diagram, we have seen that the values needed to create a chart must be contained in a worksheet. Thus, it is obvious that an existing Lotus table may be used to construct a chart.

We shall use the following exercise to become acquainted with bar charts:

Exercise 3-3: Create bar charts with different ranges, and also in stacked form

Load the TURNOVR3 file containing the real and estimated figures for the twelve months of the year.

Create a bar chart in which the real and estimated figures are represented by adjacent vertical bars. Save the diagram under the name GRAPH3.

Subsequently create a stack bar chart.

3.5.1   Bar charts with different ranges

A bar chart with different ranges is created in the same way as a line diagram. The procedure is as follows, when you have loaded the file TURNOVR3.WK1 using File Retrieve:

Selecting the type of graph

Select the type of graph using /GT. Specify the desired option, B for bar.

Specifying the ranges

Before specifying the ranges, it is advisable to enter the first letters of the months in a column G. The worksheet should appear as follows:

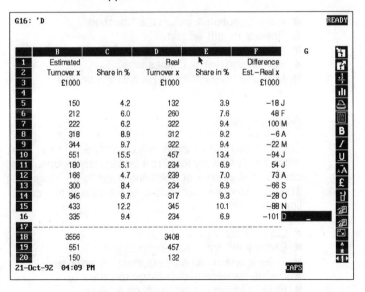

If the names of the months were written in full, the labels along the X axis would be too long.

Subsequently, the following data can be entered as range values in the Graph menu:

X range	G5..G16
A range	B5..B16
B range	D5..D16

Specifying titles

In bar charts, definition of titles is just the same as in the case of line diagrams. For the texts, the procedure is as follows in our example:

■ Go to Graph Options Titles using /GOT.
■ Select the First option.
■ Enter a main title, for instance, 'Comparison real/estimated turnover'.
■ Select the Second option and enter the subtitle 'Year 1992'.
■ Activate option X-axis in the Title menu.
■ Specify 'month' as text.
■ Activate the Y-axis option in the Title menu.
■ Specify the text 'in £ thousands'.
■ Use Quit to return to the parent menu.

Adding legends

Because two data ranges will be included in the diagram, it is necessary to add an explanatory legend. This clarifies the pattern or colouring used in the diagram. The procedure with legends is also similar to that of the line diagrams:

■ Go to Graph Options Legend.
■ Choose the first data range using A.
■ Enter a text or cell address, here: 'Estimated'.
■ Define the second data range using B.
■ Enter a text or cell address, here: 'Real'.
■ Use Quit to return to the main menu.

Displaying the diagram

You can now display the diagram using Graph View or F10:

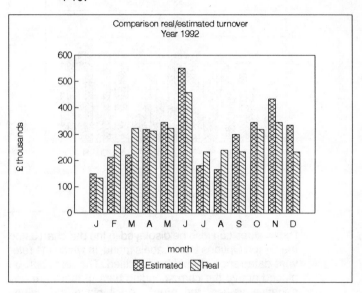

Adding gridlines and data values to bar charts

We shall now add gridlines to the bar chart. The Graph Options Grid menu is used to do this. Select the Horizontal option. The following screen is the result:

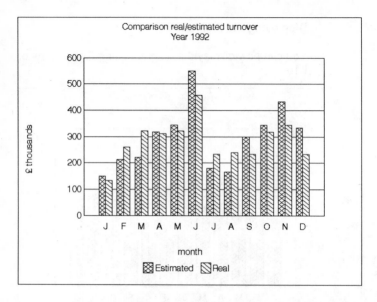

Data values can also be displayed in the bar chart using the Graph Options Data-Labels menu, in which the relevant data range should be specified. The texts can be placed above the corresponding bars. If there are any negative values, the program will place the values underneath the corresponding bar.

Scale distribution

Lotus 1-2-3 automatically makes a scale distribution and numeration along the axes in a way that allows all data to be displayed. An alternative distribution can be specified using Graph Options Scale. This provides the options X scale, Y scale and Skip. With the X and Y scales, it is possible to have the scaling done automatically or to do it yourself. Try it manually for the Y axis. Specify 1000 as the upper limit and observe the difference with the original display.

Lotus 1-2-3 ignores a positive lower limit and a negative upper limit for the X axis. Accordingly, you are assured of zero being included in the scale distribution.

The Format option allows you to determine the format of the figures for the axis display. The possible options are: Fixed, Sci (for exponential notation), Currency, General (default setting), +/-, Percent, Date (covers Time), Text and Hidden. Lengthy X labels frequently form a problem since they lead to overlapping or shortened labels. In that case, the Skip option in the Graph Options Scale can be useful. Here you can specify a factor in which the labels on the X axis should be displayed.

Applying colour and pattern

The Options command enables you to vary the colouring or, in the case of a monochrome monitor, the pattern or shading. Here, we shall deal briefly with the difference between the settings and we shall discuss the colouring and patterns more extensively in the following section which deals with pie charts.

We shall presume that the program is running in monochrome display and that both bar types, representing the real and estimated figures, are displayed in contrasting black-and-white patterns. We shall switch to colour display, since a colour monitor has been connected. We move to the Graph Options menu and select the Color option. Thus:

■ Go to Graph Options using /GO.
■ Select the Color option.
■ Use Quit (Q) to return to the Graph menu.

When you have returned to the Graph menu, select the View option. The bars in the chart are now displayed in contrasting colours. To restore the monochrome display, you have to choose the B&W option in the Graph Options menu. Quit returns you to the Graph menu.

Subsequently, save the diagram under the name GRAPH3.

3.5.2   Creating a stacked bar chart

The bar chart in the previous section shows the real and estimated values next to one another. In a stacked bar chart, the values are placed on top of one another. If, using the above data, you select the Stack-Bar option from the Graph Type menu, the chart will take on the following shape (as you can see, we have cleared the grid):

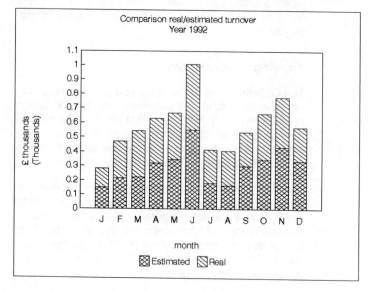

However, in our example, this is of little use.

3.5.3   Summary of section 3.5

■ There are two forms of bar charts: normal and stacked. Using the normal type, the different data ranges are displayed adjacently. In the stacked bar chart, the bars are placed above one another.

■ Choosing the type of chart is done using the Type option in the Graph menu: Bar or Stack-Bar in this case.

■ The procedure for creating bar charts corresponds to

that for creating line diagrams when determining the data ranges, titles and legends.

■ Individual values can be displayed next to the bars using the Data-Labels command from the Graph Option menu.

■ The scale distribution along the axes can be altered using the Scale option from the Graph Options menu.

■ In the case of various data ranges, the bars are displayed in different patterns or colours. Patterns are made in the case of monochrome settings and contrasting colours are displayed if there is a colour monitor. These settings are specified in the Graph Options Color menu.

3.6   Designing and creating a pie chart

Using Graph Type Pie, a chart can be created which is particularly suitable for the display of parts of a whole. The Pie is the whole, divided into various segments. The pie chart is not suited to the comparison of various data ranges or display of a large number of data points.

We shall illustrate the usage and possibilities of the pie chart by means of an exercise:

Exercise 3-4: Designing and creating a pie chart

Load the worksheet TURNOVR2.WK1, made in a previous exercise, which contains the real turnover for the individual months of the year. Using these values, make a normal pie chart and a chart in which the month of June is emphasized.

Save the file under the name GRAPH4.

3.6.1   Procedure for making a pie chart

In a pie chart, the X range corresponds to the labels of the various circle segments which represent the relevant values of the A range. In pie charts, the ranges C-F have no significance. If data is entered next to these options, it will be ignored in the diagram display.

To begin, load the table TURNOVR2 using File Retrieve. Then activate the Graph menu and choose Type, then Pie. Subsequently, the A range should be allocated the returns values and the X range should receive the texts which correspond to these values. Proceed as follows:

■ Go to the Graph Type menu using /GT.
■ Select the Pie option.
■ Select A and specify the range B4..B15.
■ Select X and specify the range A4..A15.
■ Confirm using Enter.

The range can be specified by moving the cursor to the cell where the range is to begin, anchoring it by pressing the period key and then moving to the last cell of the range. After confirmation using Enter, the range is determined.

To check this, return to the Graph menu and, using View, display the diagram on the screen. As you will observe, the percentages in the diagram are automatically calculated and displayed. Go to Graph Options Titles to enter a two-line title above the diagram:

First title: Specification of turnover per month
Second title: (1992)

The options for the titles for the X and Y axes have no meaning in a pie chart.

Display on the screen will produce the following result.

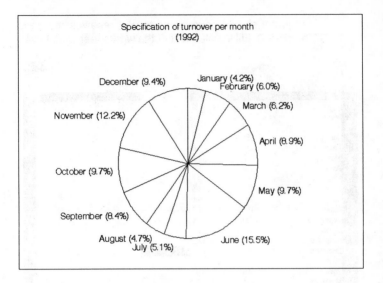

3.6.2 Designing a pie chart

Lotus 1-2-3 provides various possibilities for the design of the pie chart. The B range is used for this.

Possible options are:

■ giving patterns (shading) or colours to circle segments
■ lifting a circle segment.

Allocating patterns or colours to the circle segments

In order to allocate patterns or colours to segments, the segments must first be given appropriate code numbers in a column of the worksheet. This range of the worksheet must then be specified as the B range in the Graph menu.

Patterns can be made using the code numbers 1-7. If a

segment should have no pattern, it receives the code
number 0. Fill in column D of the worksheet as follows:

D15: 7						READY
	A	**B**	**C**	**D**	**E**	**F**
1		Turnover x	Share in %			
2	Month	£1000				
3						
4	January	150	4.2	1		
5	February	212	6.0	0		
6	March	222	6.2	2		
7	April	318	8.9	0		
8	May	344	9.7	3		
9	June	551	15.5	0		
10	July	180	5.1	4		
11	August	166	4.7	0		
12	September	300	8.4	5		
13	October	345	9.7	0		
14	November	433	12.2	6		
15	December	335	9.4	7		
16						
17	Total	3556	100			
18	Maximum	551				
19	Minimum	150				
20						

21-Oct-92 04:33 PM

Specify this range as the B range. Then display the diagram using Graph View. This should produce the following screen:

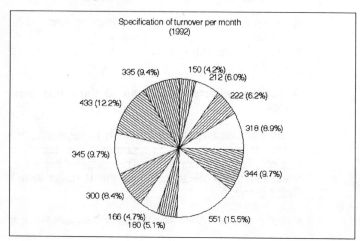

Specification of turnover per month
(1992)

335 (9.4%)   150 (4.2%)
212 (6.0%)
433 (12.2%)   222 (6.2%)
318 (8.9%)
345 (9.7%)
344 (9.7%)
300 (8.4%)
166 (4.7%)   551 (15.5%)
180 (5.1%)

Emphasizing a particular segment

According to the exercise, we should lift a certain segment out of the chart. This is also called 'exploding'. To do this, it is again necessary to specify a certain code in the worksheet. This code number must be increased by 100. From this you can conclude that codes greater than 100 lift a segment out of the pie and codes smaller than 100 display the segments attached.

Now enter the number 100 for the month of June in the worksheet. Graph View should produce the following result:

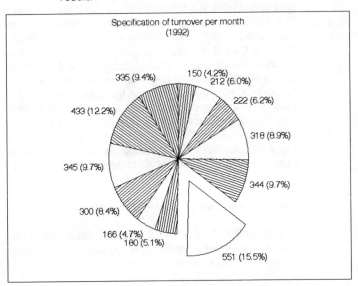

3.6.3 Summary of section 3.6

- A pie chart is especially suited to the display of a whole, subdivided into various segments.
- In a pie chart, the X range is used for the texts which should be placed next to the various circle segments. The A range contains the corresponding values.

- In a pie chart, the various segments may be allocated certain patterns (shading) or colours. To do this, an apart column containing code numbers must be entered in the worksheet. This must be defined as the B range.
- Code numbers from 1-7 are possible.
- Segments may also be lifted out of the circle. To do this, the code number must be increased by 100.

3.7   Creating XY charts

XY charts are similar to line diagrams in certain respects. In these, the X range defines the X coordinates. The Y coordinates are the values which are allocated to the ranges A to F. Each pair of XY coordinates determines a data point which is generally displayed as a symbol. These charts are particularly useful in cases where representation of dependence between two units is required. An example of this is the dependence of the returns on the advertising costs or the interwoven relationship between consumption and savings patterns.

We shall carry out the following exercise to become familiar with the creation of XY charts.

Exercise 3-5: Designing and creating an XY chart

Create an XY chart which displays the relationship between consumption expenditure and saving, depending on the available income:

Income	Expenditure	Savings
0	20	-20
50	60	-10
100	100	0
150	140	10
200	180	20

Enter the data in a Lotus 1-2-3 worksheet. Subsequently, create an XY chart with the following titles:

Main title: Consumption and savings function
X axis: Income
Y axis: Consumption/Savings

Enter the values at the appropriate points.

Save the file under the name GRAPH5.

Of course, the table must first be constructed in a worksheet of Lotus 1-2-3. That will appear as follows:

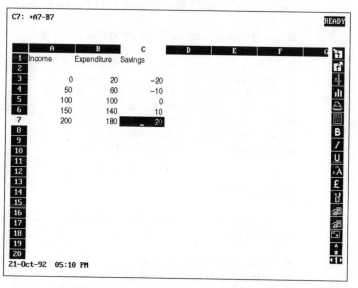

Creating an XY chart is similar to constructing a line diagram. The most important difference is that, in the case of an XY chart, the X axis is not an explanation, but always contains number values. The procedure in the example is as follows:

■ Go to the Graph Type menu using /GT.
■ Select the XY option using X.

Defining the range

The following data can be entered for the ranges in the Graph menu.

X range: A3..A7
A range: B3..B7
B range: C3..C7

Defining titles

Proceed as follows when defining titles for the chart:

- Go to Graph Options Titles using /GOT.
- Select First using F.
- Specify the main title: 'Consumption and savings function'.
- Select the option X-Axis from the same menu.
- Specify the title for the X axis: 'Income'.
- Now select the option for the Y axis: Y.
- Specify as text: 'Consumption/Savings'.
- Use Quit to return to the parent menu.

Adding a legend

Since there are two data ranges in the chart, it is necessary to add some clarification.

- Go to Graph Options Legend.
- Define the first data range with A.
- Enter a text or cell address, here: Consumption.
- Define the second data range with B.
- Enter a text or cell address, here: Savings.
- Use Q (Quit) to return to the main menu.

Adding data values to the XY chart

Data values can also be shown in an XY chart. This takes place using the Graph Options Data-Labels menu, in which you can specify the corresponding data ranges. The labels may be placed above the lines for example.

Displaying the chart

Now display the chart on the screen using the Graph View option. The result should look like this:

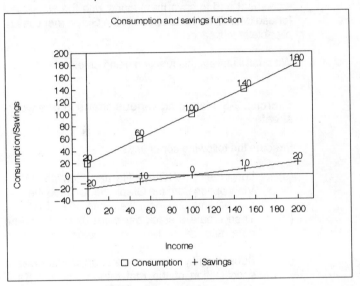

3.7.1   Summary of section 3.7

■ An XY chart is particularly suited to show the interdependence of various units.
■ In the XY chart, the X range displays the X coordinates while the values which are specified in the ranges A to F are used as the Y coordinates.
■ In the XY chart, each pair of XY coordinates determines a data point which is generally displayed as a symbol.

3.8 Managing various charts in one worksheet

In the exercises up until now, we have created charts by using a worksheet. However, when the worksheet is saved using the File Save option, only the data and parameters of the last chart are saved. It is, however, more interesting to create various charts using one worksheet and to save them along with the worksheet for use later. The Name option in the Graph menu is applicable in this case.

We shall illustrate this function using an exercise:

Exercise 3-6: Managing various charts in one worksheet

Execute the following commands:

(a)   Load the TURNOVR3 file and then select the View option from the Graph menu. Save the current parameters under the name SCREEN1.

(b)   Then create a stack bar chart using the same data and save these parameters under the name SCREEN2 using Graph Name Create.

(c)   Subsequently, make a pie chart which gives a specification of the real returns figures. Save this under the name SCREEN3.

(d)   Now activate, in succession, the charts which have been saved under the names SCREEN1 and SCREEN2.

We must first load the worksheet TURNOVR3 using File Retrieve. Then select the View option from the Graph menu. The form in which the chart was last saved, a bar chart, will then be shown.

3.8.1 Saving various charts with one worksheet

The bar chart must be saved in such a way that more charts can be made using the worksheet. These, in turn, must also be saved. Accordingly, select the Name option from the Graph menu. This will produce the following screen:

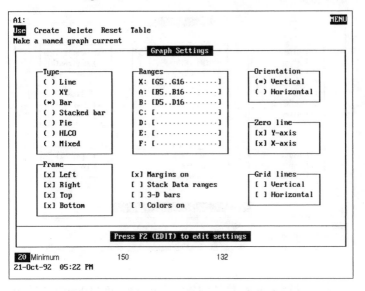

The commands in this menu have the following significance:

option	significance
Use	Selects a chart belonging to the worksheet and displays it on the screen.
Create	Names a chart in the worksheet by saving the current parameters under a specified name.
Delete	Deletes a named chart in the worksheet.
Reset	All named charts with their corresponding parameters are deleted from the worksheet.
Table	An alphabetical list of all named charts in

the worksheet is shown in three columns,
along with chart type and titles.

In order to save the first chart, we must choose the Create option. The following screen will appear:

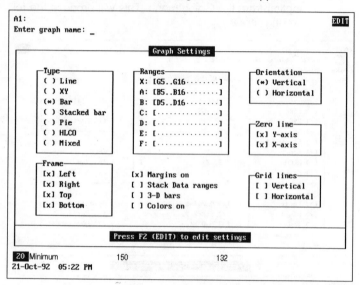

A chart name can now be specified. In this example,
this should be SCREEN1 and it may contain a maximum of 14 characters. When you have pressed Enter,
the following chart can be created. This is the stack bar
chart. To do this, you only have to alter the type and
then return to the Graph Name Create menu. Assign
the name SCREEN2 to this type. Then create the pie
chart and assign the name SCREEN3.

The procedure when allocating chart names is thus as
follows:

■ Activate the Graph menu and go to Name Create
  using /GNC.
■ Enter a name for the chart or the diagram.
■ Confirm using Enter.

If you specify an existing name, the former file will be replaced by the new one without further warning. The previous settings will also be lost. In addition, you must not forget to conclude the entire operation by saving the file using File Save in order to save the named charts along with the worksheet.

3.8.2 Displaying named charts with a worksheet

The specified chart names can be activated later using Graph Name Use. The procedure is as follows:

■ Go to Graph Name Use using /GNU.
■ Enter the name of the required chart, for instance, SCREEN1.
■ Confirm using Enter.

The result will then appear on the screen. Just as in the case of activating other files, a name can also be selected here from a list displayed, or an existing name can be entered.

3.8.3 Deleting named charts in a worksheet

It may also occur that a specified chart name has to be deleted later. The Delete option in the Graph Name menu is applicable here. The Reset option will also effect this instruction.

Using Delete, individual charts can be deleted. Specify the name of the chart when you have selected this option and press Enter. The chosen chart will be deleted immediately. The program will not request confirmation.

If you wish to delete all named charts from a worksheet in one go, select the Graph Name Reset option. The charts will also be deleted here without any request for confirmation. Only the chart which was created last will be retained.

Exercises

(1) Designing and creating a bar chart

A trading company has a sales assortment with three groups of products. The company management has the following sales figures per product group over the last six months:

Month	Product A	Product B	Product C
Jan.	320	190	444
Feb.	411	222	399
Mar.	433	238	410
Apr.	394	232	423
May	455	276	400
Jun.	476	240	378

In order to present a complete survey of the returns over the various product groups, the figures should be shown using a bar chart. In the bar chart, the three groups are shown next to one another.

(a)   First enter the data in a 1-2-3 worksheet.

(b)   Then create a bar chart. Use the following titles:
   – First: Sales development of the product groups
   – Second: (first half 1992)
   – X axis: months
   – Y axis: sales (in 1000)

(c)   Enter the following texts for the legends:
   – Product A
   – Product B
   – Product C

(d)   Display the result on the screen.

(e)   Save the worksheet under the name GRAPHEX1.WK1 and the chart under the name GRAPHEX1.PIC.

(f)   Make a correct printout.

(2)   **Creating and designing a pie chart**

On the American market for word processors, WordPerfect is the market leader with a share of 30%. Other important manufacturers are Microsoft with Word (22%), Ashton Tate with Multimate (12%), MicroPro with WordStar (12%) and IBM with Display Write (10%). (Source: IDC, 1991)

(a)   First make a normal pie chart.

(b)   Then make, instead of the normal pie chart, a pie chart in which the segment 'Multimate' is emphasized by lifting it and giving it a pattern (shading).

Save the file under the name GRAPHEX2.

Procedures

(1) (a) First enter the data in a 1-2-3 worksheet. The table can look like this, for instance:

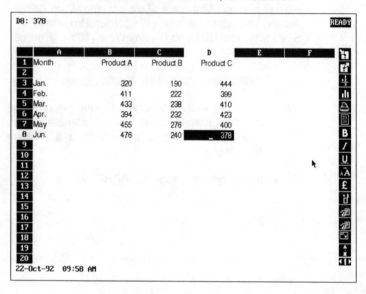

(b) Then activate the Graph menu and specify Bar. Enter the following ranges:
  – X: A3..A8
  – A: B3..B8
  – B: C3..C8
  – C: D3..D8

The required titles can be specified in Graph Options Titles.

(c) Go to Graph Options Legend to enter texts for the legend.

(d) Display the chart on the screen by selecting the View option from the Graph menu. The result should be as follows:

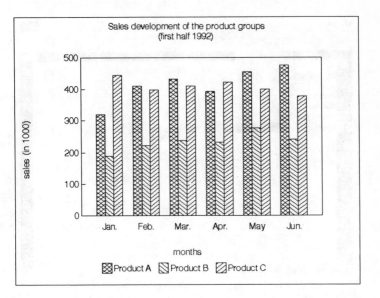

(e) Save the worksheet under the name GRAPHEX1 using the File Save command. The chart can be saved using the Graph Save option.

(f) Make a printout using the PrintGraph program.

(2) (a) First enter the data in a 1-2-3 table. Add the extra information that 14% of the market is occupied by other manufacturers. The table should appear roughly as follows:

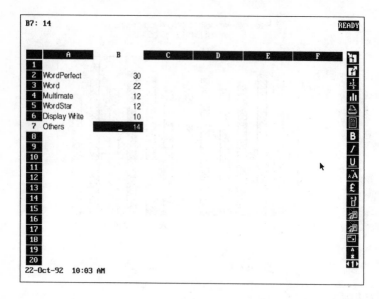

(b) Activate the Graph menu and specify Pie. Enter the names of the word processors as the X range, in this case, A2..A7. Specify the corresponding figures from B2..B7 as the A range. The result can be displayed using View. That should be as follows:

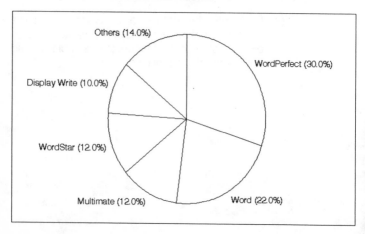

4   Data management

The third basic function in Lotus 1-2-3 concerns data management. This enables you to manage data files flexibly. For example, records can be sought and displayed if they satisfy certain criteria. In addition, versatile analysis and sorting options are available. Data from files which have been edited using the 1-2-3 database function can also be imported into Lotus 1-2-3 worksheets.

4.1   The possibilities of database programs

A database can be regarded as an extensive electronic collection of information, contrasting with the traditional information files in card indexes and folders. Electronic worksheets are used instead of card indexes for the registration of data.

In business use, database programs should be helpful in the management of extensive amounts of all sorts of data. Anyone who frequently works with large quantities of information in card indexes, catalogues or folders will recognize the value of a good database program. There are also many possibilities for application in personal situations, for example, address files or the register of a collection, such as slides, photographs, books or postage stamps.

Programs which deal with data management originated in the world of the large computer system. Due to the fact that personal computers became increasingly more powerful, these devices also became interesting for the database. Moreover, the traditional database systems on large computers cannot fulfil the requirement for information at many (work) locations at once. Databases which are oriented to the personal computer can be applied in a much more flexible way. Information in a PC database may just as easily come from the large computer as be registered at the workplace itself.

Present-day database programs for the personal computer provide the following possibilities:

- defining own files, geared to the current requirements
- quick and flexible search functions with freely chosen search criteria
- easy alteration, deletion and duplication of existing records
- formulation of reports in various ways.

In order to be able to work with a database, you must be familiar with the general structure. The following terms are important in this context:

Field   Each piece of information is entered in a field, a data field. Examples of fields in a customer file are the name of the company, the contact person, the address and the telephone number.

Record   A record is a group of data which belong together, consisting of a number of fields. Example: a collection of information about a customer, which could be useful to the user.

File   A file is comparable to a card index and consists of records which belong together. Example: all customer records together form a file.

Database   A database consists of various files. The records of these files can be connected to each other using collection criteria in such a way that they may be addressed through all the files.

4.1.1   Summary of section 4.1

- Database programs enable extensive amounts of data to be managed easily and flexibly.
- A precondition of effective usage of database programs is a suitable database structure.
- Using database programs, records can be easily found in extensive data files.
- Pertinent extracts and analyses can be made using a good database system.
- Important concepts when dealing with database programs are field, record and file.

4.2   The possibilities of the 1-2-3 database

The possibilities of the 1-2-3 database management system cannot be compared to more professional programs like dBase IV. Still, 1-2-3 can satisfy the most common requirements of smaller scale database management.

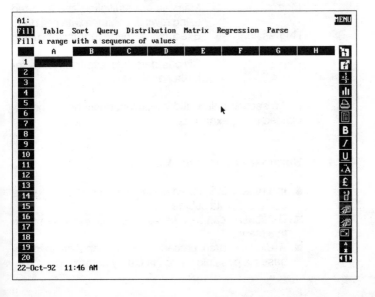

In Lotus 1-2-3, database management takes place using the Data menu. The first level of this menu is illustrated on the previous page.

These are the options available:

option	significance
Fill	This option allows fast input of a series of values in a specified range (in increasing or decreasing order).
Table	Displays the result of alteration in values within formulas in the form of a table. The table is always renewed at the moment a value in the formula is altered.
Sort	The rows in the worksheet are sorted again.
Query	Provides a record search based on certain search criteria.
Distribution	Analyzes the distribution of values in a range and calculates the frequency distribution.
Matrix	Matrices are multiplied and inverted using rows or columns with cell data.
Regression	Executes a linear regression using the current data file.
Parse	Divides data into separate cells for further analysis.

In the section below, the various instructions will be explained using examples.

4.2.1   Summary of section 4.2

■ In Lotus 1-2-3, database management takes place using the Data submenu.
■ Databases can be created using Fill and Table from this menu.
■ A direct search procedure for information in databases is possible using the Query command.

■ The options Distribution, Matrix, Regression and Parse enable you to carry out direct calculations and editing in the databases.

4.3 Creating a database in 1-2-3

In the following exercise, we shall create a database in Lotus 1-2-3:

Exercise 4-1: Create a database in Lotus 1-2-3

In a car firm, a computerized list of second-hand cars must be installed. Analogous to the card index which has been in use up until now, the following information about the second-hand cars must be registered and managed in a file:

■ make and type
■ amount of HP
■ year of manufacture
■ mileage
■ price.

In Lotus 1-2-3, a database refers to a worksheet range with data in a certain structured form, i.e. a system of records and fields. The following rules apply:

■ The record data are registered in a *worksheet row*.
■ Records consist, as mentioned, of various fields. A field is displayed in a *worksheet column*.
■ At the beginning of the database, the names of the fields must be specified in the first row. This shows which sort of information is being dealt with in the subsequent data files. It is important not to use the same name twice.

The actual data are entered in the rows under the field names. The contents of each record are related to the field name in the first row of the database. The records must be entered in the row immediately under the field name - there may be no empty rows between the field name and the records.

■ In Lotus 1-2-3, a database may contain a maximum of 256 fields, due to the fact that a worksheet contains no more than 256 columns.

4.3.1   Defining and entering fields

In the example, we must first examine the fields to be entered and their names. We shall apply the following names:

■ Make
■ HP
■ Year
■ Mileage
■ Price.

We shall first begin with a completely new worksheet. The various field names are then entered in the first row of the worksheet. The result should look something like this:

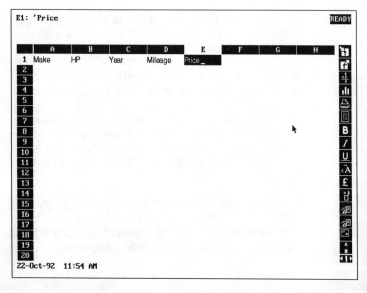

Because all records in a file have the same format, the structure of the record only needs to be specified once per file. Adjust the column width by specifying the following width for the appropriate columns using the Worksheet Column menu:

Make	20
HP	5
Year	10
Mileage	12
Price	10

The result should appear as follows:

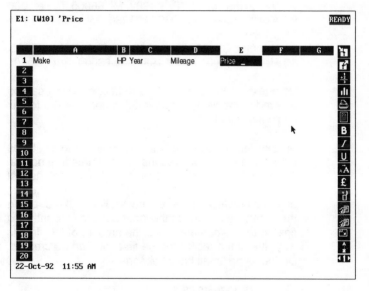

Right-align the labels in cells B1..E1.

4.3.2   Entering the data

We shall use the following information:

Exercise 4-2: Registering the records

The car firm has the following second-hand cars for sale:

1   BMW 324 d, 63 HP, Y 1987, ML 22000, Price 19000
2   Ford Fiesta, 55 HP, Y 1986, ML 25000, Price 6000
3   Ford Fiesta, 40 HP, Y 1984, ML 44000, Price 4000
4   Ford Capri, 90 HP, Y 1984, ML 64500, Price 7000
5   Mercedes 190 D, 66 HP, Y 1985, ML 37320, Price 15000
6   Mercedes 190 E, 90 HP, Y 1986, ML 22000, Price 17000
7   VW Scirocco, 70 HP, Y 1982, ML 66005, Price 7000
8   VW Scirocco, 110 HP, Y 1986, ML 38000, Price 14000
9   VW Golf GL, 50 HP, Y 1982, ML 55000, Price 6000
10 Renault R4, 35 HP, Y 1982, ML 63000, Price 3000

Both texts (labels) and values (numerical data) can be entered in the fields. However, it is not possible to mix texts and values.

In general, the input of records in a database takes place in the same way as the input of data in a normal worksheet. Accordingly, place the cell pointer at the first entry field, in this case A2. Subsequently, make the first entry immediately under the name: BMW 324 d. Using the right cursor, confirm the input and move to the next field at the same time. Enter the amount of HP. In this way, the entire record for the first sort can be created. Do the same for all the other sorts.

The result appears as follows:

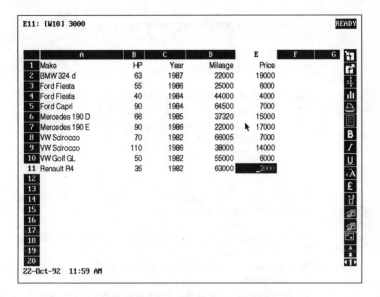

```
E11: [W10] 3000                                              READY

         A           B      C         D            E        F      G
  1  Make           HP     Year    Mileage       Price
  2  BMW 324 d      63     1987     22000         19000
  3  Ford Fiesta    55     1986     25000         6000
  4  Ford Fiesta    40     1984     44000         4000
  5  Ford Capri     90     1984     64500         7000
  6  Mercedes 190 D 66     1985     37320         15000
  7  Mercedes 190 E 90     1986     22000         17000
  8  VW Scirocco    70     1982     66005         7000
  9  VW Scirocco    110    1986     38000         14000
 10  VW Golf GL     50     1982     55000         6000
 11  Renault R4     35     1982     63000         3000
 12
 13
 14
 15
 16
 17
 18
 19
 20
22-Oct-92  11:59 AM
```

Now save the worksheet with the database under the
name SECCAR1 using the File Save command.

4.3.3   Summary of section 4.3

■ The field names should be placed in a worksheet row
   at the beginning of database made using Lotus 1-2-3.
   Each name occupies one column.
■ A record is registered in one row of the worksheet.
■ The data are entered in the usual way: go first to the
   required field using the cell pointer and then enter a
   text or value.

4.4   Retrieving records

With the Lotus 1-2-3 database, it is possible to look for a
particular record so that certain information can be re-
trieved quickly. We shall illustrate this using the following example:

Exercise 4-3: Retrieving records

During the course of the day, certain information is requested by interested parties:

(a)   Is there a Mercedes 190 D for sale?
(b)   Which types of Ford are available?
(c)   How many cars have a price tag of less than five thousand pounds?
(d)   Is there a Ford Fiesta for less than five thousand pounds?

Records can be sought in 1-2-3 using the Data Query menu. This allows you to:

■ search for records in a database using particular search criteria
■ copy records from a database to another part of the database
■ specifically search for records in a way in which duplicates are automatically excluded
■ delete records in a database.

A precondition of using this menu is that an input range, a criteria range and, if necessary, an output range are defined.

4.4.1   Defining the input range

The range in a database which is to be edited or in which the search must take place is called the input range. The contents of the input range consist of field names from the database and all entered records to be examined.

Go to the Data Query menu using /DQ. The following will appear on the screen:

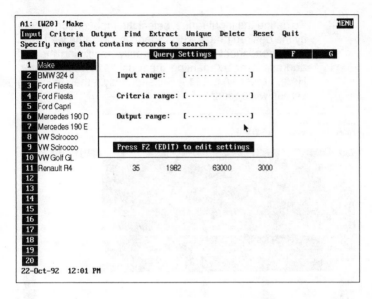

The options in this submenu have the following significance:

option	significance
Input	Defines an input range, the range with field names and records.
Criteria	Defines a criteria range.
Output	Defines a range to which the found records should be copied.
Find	Searches for particular records using specified criteria.
Extract	Copies the records which satisfy the criteria to the specified output range.
Unique	Removes all duplicate records when copying using the search criteria.
Delete	Deletes all records which satisfy certain criteria.
Reset	Deletes the data entered in the input range, the criteria range and the output range.
Quit	Returns to the READY mode.

To define the input range, select the Input option. Specify the desired range. This is done in the same way as in
the spreadsheet - either by directly specifying the cell
addresses or by marking them using the cell pointer.
Here, enter A1..E11. Subsequently, the following
screen will appear:

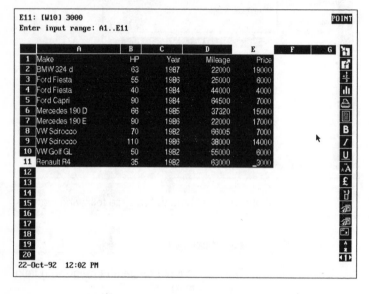

When you have confirmed the command using Enter,
the program will return to the Data menu.

The general procedure is as follows:

■ Go to the initial cell in the worksheet using the cell
  pointer.
■ Activate the Data Query menu using /DQ.
■ Select the Input option using Enter or I.
■ Specify the input range.
■ Confirm using Enter.

4.4.2 Defining the criteria range

Using the criteria range, the program is instructed how to search for certain records. The appropriate selection criteria must be defined in this criteria range. These criteria may refer to a single field or to several fields in a database at once. In the latter case, various combinations can also be made.

An empty range within the worksheet should be used in which there is sufficient space for the specification of the criteria. It is advisable to situate the range several cells to the right or underneath the actual database.

In our example, we shall choose cell A30 as the starting point for the criteria range. In the first row of the criteria range, the database field names which will serve as selection criteria must be specified. The simplest way is to copy the row containing the field names, row 1, to row 30, so that the following screen will be produced:

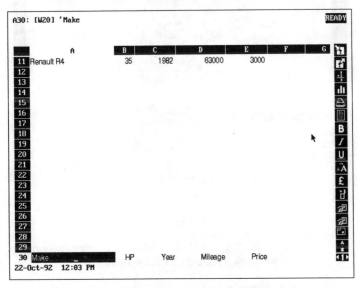

It is certainly not necessary to specify all the field names here. The field names which will be checked later against the criterion are important. This means that in the first row of the criteria range only one particular field name or a part of all field names will be entered.

In the criteria range, the appropriate selection criteria should be specified in the following row. Here, it is important to place the selection criterion exactly underneath the corresponding field name.

In our example, there is a request concerning the availability of a certain make. Therefore, something must be entered in the first column under the Make field. Since the request deals with a certain sort, the make and type can be specified in this field. The screen should look like this:

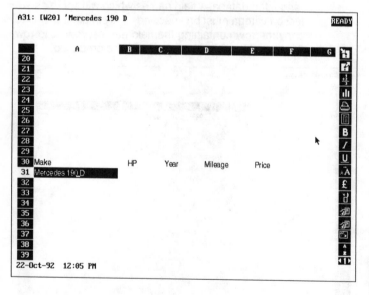

When entering selection criteria in the criteria range, the following rules should be kept in mind:

■ If a certain text is sought which must conform precisely to the criterion, you must specify the exact text.

- It is also possible to search for a certain value which conforms exactly to the specified criterion.
- A formula can also be a criterion. Then, it is advisable to to make the desired formula visible using /RFT.
- Various criteria are possible simultaneously. If records which fulfil all criteria have to be sought, the different criteria must be entered in the same row. However, if the records only have to satisfy one of the criteria, the different criteria should each be placed in a separate row.

When the data have been entered in the criteria range, the range can be defined. Go to the Data Query Criteria menu and specify the relevant range. In our example, that is A30..E31. The result is as follows:

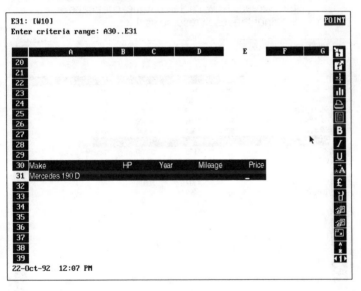

Thus, the definition of a criteria range takes place as follows, presuming that a copy of the field names has already been made in row 30:

- Using the cursor keys, go to the field for the selection criterion, here A31.

- Specify the criterion, here Mercedes 190 D.
- Go to Data Query Criteria using /DQC.
- Specify the criteria range, here A30..E31.
- Confirm the command using Enter.

When this command has been carried out, the program returns to the Data Query menu.

4.4.3   Searching in the database

We shall now implement the search procedure using the specified criterion, i.e. using the Find command from Data Query. Records which satisfy the specified criterion when the command is executed are highlighted on the screen. Now implement the command and check whether the result resembles this:

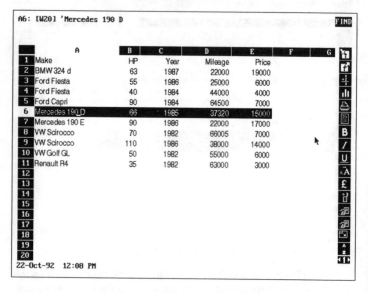

The result shows that there is indeed a Mercedes of the desired type for sale. The record which is found using the selection criterion is highlighted. Of course, it may occur that more records fulfil the selection criterion. In that case, you can use the cursor down key to move to the other records. The program will automatically direct you to the records found, until there are no more records which satisfy the specified criterion. The program then gives a signal and returns to the Query menu.

The following list outlines the significance of the various keys in the Data Query Find menu:

key	significance
cursor down	Shows the next record which fulfils the selection criterion.
cursor up	Shows the previous record which fulfils the selection criterion.
cursor right	Moves the cell pointer one field to the right within the highlighted record.
cursor left	Moves the cell pointer one field to the left within the highlighted record.

In our example, only one record satisfies our criterion. Accordingly, a signal is given as soon as we attempt to move the cursor downwards. The search procedure is terminated by pressing Enter. The program then returns to the Query menu.

If you then save the worksheet, the input and criteria ranges last specified are also saved. Save the file under the name SECCAR1. You can thus make use of the specified settings later.

Using F7, the Query key, you are able to quickly execute the previous search instruction again from the READY mode.

4.4.4 Special details when selecting records

In the first example, we sought a certain type of car. For that reason, the label was entered just as it occurs in the database. It is only possible to reach an exact correspondence in that way.

However, it regularly happens that the exact formulation is not precisely known or that texts or values which are located in a certain range have to be found. For these cases, there are special rules. We shall illustrate these using an example. There may be special criteria in the following areas in the car trade:

- Various makes have to be found.
- The required car must be within a certain price class.
- The required record must fulfil different criteria.

Before entering new criteria, remember to remove the previous criteria first. This takes place in the Range Erase menu, in which the relevant cell address should be specified. Subsequently, enter the desired selection criteria for the new request.

Comparison of criteria using special characters

The second question in the present example deals with the request for all Ford models. Accordingly, 'ford*' must be specified in field A31. By entering an asterisk, a wildcard is used to represent a longer text. Each random character from the fifth position onwards is assumed to belong to the selection criterion. If you now begin the search procedure using Data Query Find, you will see the screen shown on page 215.

If you move the cursor downwards, it will be obvious that three types of Ford are for sale. Only the available Fords are displayed. Subsequently an acoustic signal is given to indicate that no more records which satisfy these criteria have been found.

The following special characters can be used in the search procedure:

- The **asterisk** is a wildcard for a longer text.
- The **question mark** is a wildcard for any one character.
- A **tilde** (~) in front of the criterion ensures that the

criterion is reversed. If the selection criterion is '~ford'
for instance, those records which do not contain information concerning 'Ford' will be displayed. This can
be a useful criterion, for example, if a buyer arrives
who wishes anything but a Ford.

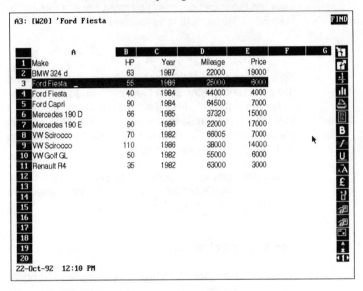

Values and formulas as criterion

Often records are sought which contain certain values
or in which the values are located in a certain value
range. That is no problem in Lotus 1-2-3.

It is possible to formulate selection criteria using certain
values. In as much as an exact correspondence with a
value is desired, only this value need be specified as
the selection criterion in the appropriate cell.

It is different if a conditional correspondence is required.
In this case, the selection criterion uses a logical ex-
pression as a condition. In this, operators, with which
you are already familiar from the spreadsheet, are ap-

plied. The formula must be constructed in such a way
that a cell address is compared to a random other
value.

For instance, if you wish to know which cars cost less
than ten thousand pounds, you must enter a formula in
field E31. The formula is as follows:

```
+E2<10000
```

This criterion E2<10000 activates the program, using
the commands in the Data Query menu, to find all records with a price of less than ten thousand pounds. If
you enter the formula in the worksheet, a zero will first
appear. Using the Text option from Range Format, you
can make the formulas visible.

When the formula is placed in the cell, you can check
the result using Data Query Find. If everything has gone
smoothly, six records should be found.

Combination of criteria

As mentioned, various criteria may be applied at once.
We shall examine the possibilities using the following
example. In this, two simultaneous criteria must be fulfilled. Since the required records must satisfy both criteria, they must be placed in the same row. Lotus 1-2-3
deals with criteria entered in one row as if they are connected using the #AND# operator.

When the data have been removed from the range, the
following should be entered:

```
A31: Ford Fiesta
E31: +E2<5000
```

This produces the following screen:

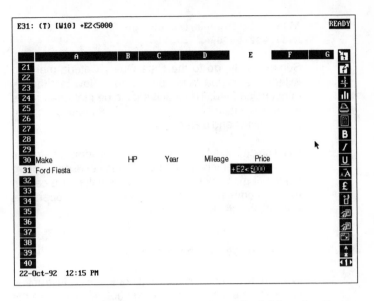

As mentioned, the formula is made visible using Range Format Text.

As you carry out the search procedure, it will become obvious that when criteria are entered in different fields of a single row, the program connects all data using the #AND# operator. In the example in question, all types of Ford Fiesta which cost less than five thousand pounds will be selected. The result can only be one record, that in row 4. You can check this by implementing Data Query Find.

OR connections are also possible in the database. This concerns records which fulfil one of the criteria. In that case, the different criteria must always be entered in a separate row.

Imagine that we are searching for cars which are either Ford Fiestas or cost less than five thousand pounds. When the current data have been removed from the range in E31, we can then enter:

```
A31: Ford Fiesta (no change)
E32: +E2<5000
```

Subsequently, go to the Data Query Criteria menu to extend the criteria range by one row. Now test the request using Find. The result should be that three types are found which conform to the #OR# application, two Ford Fiestas and a Renault 4.

It is also possible to specify constructed logical formulas in a field as selection criterion. This is necessary, for instance, if more than one condition is valid for a certain field. A combination can be made using the operators #AND#, #OR# and #NOT#.

4.4.5   Output of search commands

We can also transport the result of a search instruction to a separate range of the worksheet. We shall use the previous example to do this.

Before we can implement the instruction, we must first define the output range. Go to an empty part of the worksheet and ensure that the range which is to be specified does not overlap the input or criteria range. In particular, there must also be sufficient space to accept records. A good spot is several rows under the actual database or the criteria range which has been defined there.

In this example, we shall choose row 40. On the first row of the output range, just as with the criteria range, you should place the field names which are to be used for the selection criteria. The easiest way to place them there is to copy the row containing the field names of the criteria range to the desired row for the output range. The maximum number of fields for an output range is 32.

Then you can define the output range by activating Data Query Output. Specify the range here. For instance,

you can specify A40..E45, but A40..E40 is also sufficient. In the latter case, there are no limits for the output
of records found. The rows underneath will be automatically deleted. In the first case, you limit the output to
five rows. If there are six records which satisfy the criterion, the program will produce an error message.

The actual output of the selected records to the defined
range can now take place. Select the Extract option
from the Data Query menu. The result should appear as
follows:

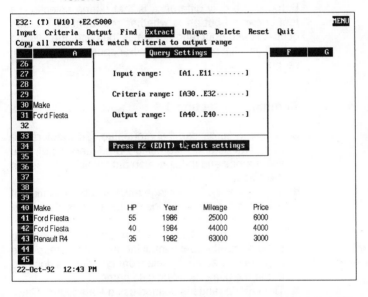

The figure shows that all records selected using the
command have been copied to the specified range.

A concise summary of the procedure:

■ Enter a criterion in the criteria range.
■ Using /C, copy the field names of the criteria range to
the output range.
■ Using /DQO, go to the Data Query Output menu.
■ Define the output range, for example A40..E40.

■ Select the Extract option.

If you wish to completely renew the search in a database and you wish to be sure that no data from previous instructions are accidentally included, you should make use of the Reset option in the Data Query menu. This removes all data concerning input-, criteria- and output ranges in the worksheet.

In addition, you will see the Unique option in the Data Query menu. This option is, in principle, the same as Extract. The only difference is that during selection, a test is carried out as to whether two identical records occur in the output range. If that is the case, the second record is eliminated prior to transport to the output range.

4.4.6   Summary of section 4.4

■ Before records can be requested, an input range must first be specified using Data Query Input. The field names and the specified data which are used in the selection are placed here.
■ In addition, a criteria range must also be specified. It is best to have this outside the data range. This contains the field names which are used to make the selection criteria. The selection criteria are placed underneath the row containing the field names. It is important that each selection criterion is located under the corresponding field name.
■ The criteria range is defined using Data Query Criteria.
■ The actual search procedure takes place using the Find command from the Data Query menu. If there are more records which satisfy the selection criteria, they can be made visible using the cursor down key.
■ Selection criteria may be texts and values. The asterisk and question mark can be used as wildcards. Formulas can also be used as selection criteria. They enable conditional testing.
■ To produce an apart display of the result of a search,

you must first define an output range using Data Query Output. Actual output takes place using the Extract or Unique command from the Data Query menu.

4.5   Editing records (file maintenance)

There are various situations in which it is necessary to alter or update an existing file. It may be necessary to alter the contents of a record or to delete or add a record.

We shall discuss the possibilities provided by Lotus 1-2-3 in this area using the following example.

Exercise 4-4: Editing records

The following alterations should be made to the file containing the second-hand cars:

■ Since the 55 HP Ford Fiesta cannot raise the desired price, this sum must be reduced by one thousand pounds.
■ An Opel Corsa with the following features must be added to the file: 45 HP, Year 1986, Mileage 34,000, Price eight thousand pounds.
■ The Mercedes 190 E has been sold.

In general, records are dealt with as in a spreadsheet. This applies both to making alterations and to copying and adding new records.

4.5.1   Altering the contents of a record

In order to make later alterations to the contents of records, you must first go to the appropriate record and select the desired field. You then have the following possibilities:

- You can replace the contents of the field by entering new contents.
- You can alter (edit) the contents after pressing F2.

In the example, proceed as follows to change the price of the Fiesta:

- Using the cursor keys, go to field E3.
- Enter the new price, 5,000.
- Confirm the alteration using Enter.

4.5.2   Adding records

Extra records can be inserted or added later at any row position in the database:

- Insertion takes place by first creating extra space for the insertion using Worksheet Insert Row.
- A record or row can be added to the end of a database without any problem. Keep in mind that any input range for searches using Data Query should be adjusted.

In our example, the record for the Opel Corsa should be added in row 12. Go to the end of the database and enter the data concerning the Corsa. You can switch fields using the cursor keys.

4.5.3   Deleting a record

When a car is sold, the relevant record can be removed from the database. In this case, that is the record in row 7. Direct deletion of records takes place in the Data Query Delete menu. There, you may enter selection criteria for the deletion of records in the specified input range. This is especially useful if complete records should be deleted in one go.

In the example, the procedure is as follows once the correct input range has been specified and other selection criteria, if any, have been removed:

- Go to the criteria range to specify a selection criterion. Here, that is A31.
- Specify the criterion: Mercedes 190 E.
- Go to Data Query Criteria using /DQC.
- Specify the criteria range: A30..E31.
- Confirm using Enter.
- Select the Delete option and confirm the safeguard question by choosing Delete again.

Before you confirm the deletion procedure using the Delete option, the screen looks like this:

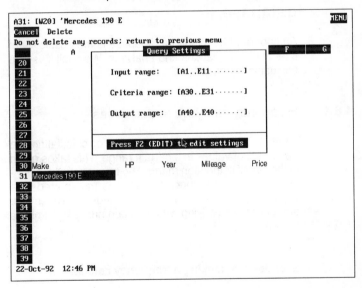

```
A31: [W20] 'Mercedes 190 E                                    MENU
Cancel  Delete
Do not delete any records; return to previous menu
           A                    Query Settings            F       G
  20
  21             Input range:    [A1..E11········]
  22
  23             Criteria range: [A30..E31········]
  24
  25             Output range:   [A40..E40········]
  26
  27
  28             Press F2 (EDIT) to edit settings
  29
  30  Make               HP      Year      Mileage      Price
  31  Mercedes 190 E
  32
  33
  34
  35
  36
  37
  38
  39
22-Oct-92  12:46 PM
```

Before the deletion instruction is actually carried out, you must first confirm it. An unintentional action can be corrected at this stage.

Now delete the Opel Corsa again and raise the price of the Fiesta to £6000 once more. Save the database again under the name SECCAR2.

4.5.4   Summary of section 4.5

- Before a record an be altered, the field to be altered must be found and the contents replaced. It is also possible to edit the contents using F2.
- If records have to be added later at a certain position, the worksheet must first be extended by one empty row using Worksheet Insert Row.
- Records can be deleted directly using Data Query Delete.

4.6   Analyses using the Lotus 1-2-3 database

An important function of a database is the possibility of executing calculations and analyses. We shall illustrate this using examples.

4.6.1   Frequency analyses in databases

Lotus 1-2-3 provides the possibility of calculating the frequency of values in a certain range. This takes place in the Data Distribution menu. The frequency of the various values in the specified range is transported to a separately specified worksheet range in which the amount of values lying within certain numerical limits is shown.

Exercise 4-5: Making a frequency calculation

When planning, it is important to know how the division of the stocks of cars into price classes will take place. In the light of a frequency analysis, the amount of cars should be calculated which:

- are cheaper than five thousand pounds;
- cost between five and ten thousand pounds;
- cost between ten and fifteen thousand pounds;

■ cost between fifteen and twenty thousand pounds;
■ are more expensive than twenty thousand pounds.

Before the actual calculation can take place, the range in which the results will be located must be defined. In this example, we shall place the results in columns G and H.

Using the cell pointer, go to cell G2 and enter the desired interval values in increasing order in the column. The screen should look like this:

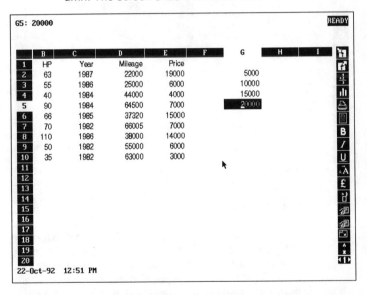

Thus, the interval data are located in the range G2..G5. This range is the left-hand column of the result worksheet and is called the frequency value range. When defining this range, keep in mind that the column to the left must be empty and that there must also be empty cells under the frequency value range.

Now activate the Data Distribution menu and enter the necessary data. You must first specify the values range containing the values to be analyzed, in our example

that is E2..E11. Then specify the 'bin' range. This is
G2..G5. In the analysis, only the number values are cal-
culated. Labels and empty cells are ignored.
The result is as follows:

G5: 20000									READY
	B	**C**	**D**	**E**	**F**	G	**H**	**I**	
1	HP	Year	Mileage	Price					
2	63	1987	22000	19000		5000	2		
3	55	1986	25000	6000		10000	4		
4	40	1984	44000	4000		15000	2		
5	90	1984	64500	7000		20000	1		
6	66	1985	37320	15000			0		
7	70	1982	66005	7000					
8	110	1986	38000	14000					
9	50	1982	55000	6000					
10	35	1982	63000	3000					
11									
12									
13									
14									
15									
16									
17									
18									
19									
20									
22-Oct-92 12:54 PM									

You will observe in the figure that the results of the calculations are placed in the column to the right of the frequency values. You can see how and to what extent the
data from the value range fall inside the limits of the
diverse intervals. The quantity corresponds to the
amount of values in the specified range which is greater
than the previous frequency value but is not greater
than the actual value (in column G). In addition, the
number of values greater than the largest interval value
is shown in an extra cell. In our example that is 0 since
there is no car costing more than twenty thousand
pounds.

Summarizing, the procedure is as follows, after the interval values have been specified in the worksheet:

■ Go to the Data Distribution menu using /DD.

■ Specify the value range E2..E11.
■ Specify the frequency value range (bin range) G2..G5.
■ Confirm using Enter.

Subsequently save the database under the name SEC-CAR3 using File Save.

4.6.2 Calculations using database functions

In Lotus 1-2-3, it is possible to calculate average minimum and maximum values. This may be required, for instance, when a selection has taken place, i.e. a request based on certain criteria. At such moments, the statistical functions of the program can be extremely useful.

We shall apply these functions using the following example:

Exercise 4-6: Calculations using statistical database functions

When planning, it can be important to make statistical analyses of a database. Load the SECCAR2 file and examine which makes of car cost more than five thousand pounds. Have the program calculate the following:

■ the number of selected values
■ the total value of the selected cars
■ the average value of the selected cars
■ the highest price
■ the lowest price

First load the file using File Retrieve. Then go to the criteria range and place the following formula in cell E31:

+E2>5000

Check whether the input and criteria ranges have been correctly defined and then implement the Data Query Find command.

You can now construct a database range. Increase the column width of H to twenty characters and enter the text data. The input should take place in the range H2..H6.

The corresponding formulas must be placed in column I. Enter the following formula for the number of selected cars:

```
@DCOUNT(A1..E10,4,A30..E31)
```

Explanation of this formula:

- The first argument between brackets concerns the input range of the database. This deals with the field names and specified records.
- Subsequently, the column number of the field in which the analysis takes place must be specified. In our example, this is the fourth column from the left, where the price is stated.
- The range in which the criterion is located should be given as the criteria range, the last argument between brackets.

In the same way, enter the remaining formulas in the rows 3 to 6 of column I. When everything has been filled in, the screen should appear as follows:

```
I6: @DMIN(A1..E10,4,A30..E31)                                    READY
```

	D	E	F	G	H	I
1	Mileage	Price				
2	22000	19000			Number:	7
3	25000	6000			Total value	74000
4	44000	4000			Average value	10571.42
5	64500	7000			Highest price	19000
6	37320	15000			Lowest price	6000
7	66005	7000				
8	38000	14000				
9	55000	6000				
10	63000	3000				
11						
12						
13						
14						
15						
16						
17						
18						
19						
20						

22-Oct-92 01:09 PM

4.6.3 Summary of section 4.6

- Using the Data Frequency instruction, it is possible to calculate the amount of records which fall within a specified range in a database range of values.
- A precondition of efficient usage of the Data Frequency instruction is the definition of an interval range in a free area of the worksheet. This is called the frequency value area.
- When the Data Frequency command has been implemented, the results are displayed in the column next to the frequency value range.
- Using the database functions, various statistical calculations can be carried out in a database. That can also be done after commands have been carried out using Data Query.

4.7 Sorting records

In principle, records entered in Lotus 1-2-3 are saved in the order of sequence in which they were registered.

However, it may be desirable to sort the records in alphabetical or numerical order - for instance, alphabetical according to make or numerical according to price.

In Lotus 1-2-3, this rearrangement takes place using the Data Sort menu, in which a specification of the information can be made. The Data Sort submenu looks like this:

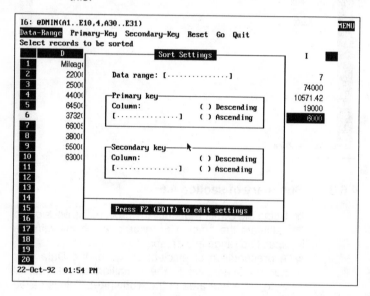

The following exercise will illustrate exactly how sorting occurs.

Exercise 4-7: Sorting records

The file containing the second-hand cars SECCAR2 must be sorted for calculation purposes in this way:

■ in alphabetical order according to make
■ according to price (most expensive first) within make classification.

First activate the Data-Range option from the Data Sort submenu. Here you will be asked to specify the range to be sorted, in this case A2..E10. In contrast to the previous commands, the row containing the field names (A1..E1) may not be specified.

Then select the Primary-Key option. The screen will appear as follows:

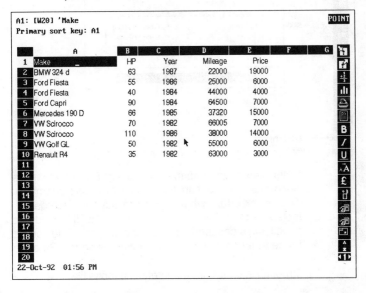

First, you must specify the cell which will serve as the primary sorting criterion, in our example A1. After confirmation using Enter, you must specify the order of sortation. This can be Ascending or Descending. In our example, we shall select A for Ascending. The screen now appears as follows:

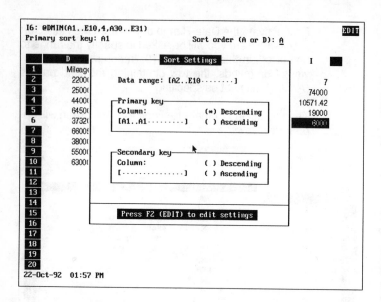

When you have confirmed this using Enter, select the Secondary-Key option from the Data Sort submenu. This is important when there are several records selected by the primary key. Now we shall fill in field E1, specifying a descending order of sequence. The sorting procedure can now be set in motion using the Go command from the Data Sort menu. The result of the instruction is shown immediately and looks like this:

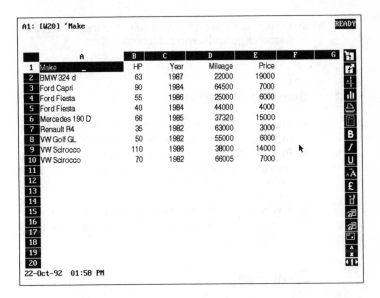

```
A1: [W20] 'Make                                                    READY

          A            B      C        D        E      F      G
 1  Make        _      HP     Year    Mileage   Price
 2  BMW 324 d          63     1987    22000     19000
 3  Ford Capri         90     1984    64500     7000
 4  Ford Fiesta        55     1986    25000     6000
 5  Ford Fiesta        40     1984    44000     4000
 6  Mercedes 190 D     66     1985    37320     15000
 7  Renault R4         35     1982    63000     3000
 8  VW Golf GL         50     1982    55000     6000
 9  VW Scirocco        110    1986    38000     14000
10  VW Scirocco        70     1982    66005     7000
11
12
13
14
15
16
17
18
19
20
22-Oct-92  01:58 PM
```

The records are now arranged in such a way that they
are shown in ascending order of sequence, based on
the primary sort key. In cases where there are two ve-
hicles of the same make, the more expensive one is
placed before the cheaper one.

A summary of the procedure:

■ Go to Data Sort using /DS.
■ Select the Data-Range option using Enter or D.
■ Define the range A2..E10.
■ Select the Primary-Key option using P.
■ Enter A1 (make) as the primary sort key.
■ Specify Ascending (A) as the order of sequence.
■ Select the Secondary-Key option using S.
■ Specify the field E1 (price) as the secondary sort key.
■ Define the sort order as Descending using D.
■ Execute the command using the instruction Go.

Finally, here are a couple of remarks about the remaining options in the Data Sort menu.

■ Using the Reset option, all parameters in Data Sort (data range sort keys) can be cancelled.
■ Return to the READY mode using Quit.

4.7.1   Summary of section 4.7

■ The Data Sort instruction enables you to arrange the records of a database in another order of sequence.
■ Prior to this rearrangement, a data range must be specified containing only the records which are to be sorted. The field names may not be included in this range.
■ Two sort keys can be specified simultaneously.
■ The actual sort procedure is set in motion using the Go command from the Data Sort menu.

Exercises

(1)   Create a customer file and enter the following information about the customers:

Cst.nr	Name	Street	PC	Town	Turnover
1455	Fagan Ltd.	7 Purse St.	L14 3AB	London	80,000
1742	Twist Ltd.	18 Soho	L17 2AB	London	420,000
1940	Bumble Ltd.	9 Beadle Ave.	NO2 8EQ	Nottingham	45,000
2959	Copperfield Ltd.	1 Beech Lane	BA2 3CD	Bath	345,450
4508	Dorrit Ltd.	6 Little Drive	MA5 6OT	Manchester	185,000
6500	Marley Ltd.	2 Rack Road	DV4 5TD	Dover	234,599

(2)   Specify the relevant criteria for the following applications and subsequently check them:

(a) all customers who live in London
(b) the address data of Bumble Ltd.
(c) all customer numbers less than 4000
(d) all customers with a turnover of less than 100,000 pounds.

(3)   Sort the database according to turnover figures and save the file under the name CUSTOMRS.

Solutions

(1)   Firstly, enter the field names in one row of the worksheet. Each field name requires one column in the worksheet, making a total of six. Then enter the records one by one, each record in its own row. Proceed as you always do: first go to the desired cell with the cell pointer, enter the text or value and move to the next cell using the cursor keys.

(2)   The following selection criteria should be made:

   (a) in the 'Town' column: London
   (b) in the 'Name' column: Bumble Ltd.
   (c) in the 'Cst.nr' column: +A2<4000
   (d) In the 'Turnover' column: +F2>100000

(3)   Proceed as follows:

   – Activate Data Sort using /DS.
   – Select the Data-Range option using Enter or D.
   – Define the range: A2..F7.
   – Select the Primary-Key option using P.
   – Specify the 'Turnover' field, F1.
   – Choose the Descending sort order using D.
   – Implement the command using Go.

   The result should be as follows:

A1: [W5] 'Cst.nr   READY

	A	B	C	D	E	F
1	Cst.nr	Name	Street	PC	Town	Turnover
2	1742	Twist Ltd.	18 Soho	L17 2AB	London	420,000
3	2959	Copperfield Ltd.	1 Beech Lane	BA2 3CD	Bath	345,450
4	6500	Marley Ltd.	2 Rack Road	DV4 5TD	Dover	234,599
5	4508	Dorrit. Ltd.	6 Little Drive	MA5 6OT	Manchester	185,000
6	1455	Fagan Ltd.	7 Purse Street	L14 3AB	London	80,000
7	1940	Burnble Ltd.	9 Beadle Ave.	NO2 8EQ	Nottingham	45,000
8						
9						
10						
11						
12						
13						
14						
15						
16						
17						
18						
19						
20						

22-Oct-92   02:09 PM

5 Exchange with other programs and Add-ins

In daily practice, various programs are used simultaneously in many businesses. In addition to spreadsheets, word processors and database programs are also commonly in use. Recognizing this fact, Lotus 1-2-3 provides the possibility of exchanging data with other programs. There are two possibilities in this respect:

■ direct adoption of files from other programs
■ conversion of files using the utility program Translate.

5.1 Direct import of files

Lotus 1-2-3 is able to directly import files in the ASCII format. They can be adopted in the current 1-2-3 worksheet using the Import command from the File menu and are then immediately available for editing. In this way, text from word processors can be imported, as long as it has been saved in ASCII format in the original program.

For instance, if you wish to import the text file TEXTXY in 1-2-3, proceed as follows:

■ Go to the File menu and select the Import option using /FI.
■ Select one of the options Text or Numbers, Text in this case.
■ Specify the name of the file: TEXTXY.

When you have pressed Enter, the text will appear on the screen. Any layout of the text will be lost and operating characters may appear on the screen. The imported text will, thus, require editing and layout.

5.2 Exchange of data using the utility program Translate

The Translate utility program belongs to the Lotus package. This enables you to exchange data with other programs. This means that it is possible to export Lotus files to other programs for further processing and to import files for further usage in Lotus 1-2-3.

In both cases, you must first activate the Translate utility program. This can be done in the Access menu and also directly from the DOS instruction line by typing 'trans'. The following screen will appear:

```
              Lotus  1-2-3  Release 2.4 Translate Utility
  Copr. 1985, 1991, 1992  Lotus Development Corporation  All Rights Reserved


What do you want to translate FROM?

        1-2-3 1A
        1-2-3 2 through 2.2
        1-2-3 2 through 2.4
        1-2-3 2.3, 2.4 WK1/FMT
        dBase II
        dBase III
        DIF
        Enable 2.0
        Multiplan (SYLK)
        SuperCalc4
        Symphony 1.0
        Symphony 1.1 through 2.2
        VisiCalc

        Move the menu pointer to your selection and press ENTER
              Press ESC to end the Translate utility
              Press F1 (HELP) for more information
```

5.2.1 Exporting Lotus files

If a Lotus file is to be exported to another program, this file is the source file and 1-2-3 the source program. Accordingly, when the initial screen appears, select the proper version of 1-2-3 and press Enter.

A possible application is, for example, the export of the file to a database program such as dBase for further processing of the data. To do this, you must, in the subsequent step, specify the desired target program, for example, dBase III. When you have pressed Enter, remarks will be displayed on the screen concerning the chosen translation. Press Esc and the following screen will appear:

```
                Lotus  1-2-3  Release 2.4 Translate Utility
   Copr. 1985, 1991, 1992  Lotus Development Corporation  All Rights Reserved


   Translate FROM: 1-2-3 2.4              Translate TO: dBase III

   Source file: C:\123R24\*.WK1

    APPRENT  WK1  10/21/92   2:19p      2860

            APPRENT  WK1
            BREAK    WK1
            CAPVALUE WK1
            COLORTST WK1
            COMMISSN WK1
            COSTEFF  WK1
            COSTS    WK1
            —More—


   Move the menu pointer to the file you want to translate and press ENTER
            Press ESC to edit the source file specification
                Press F1 (HELP) for more information
```

Now choose the required file using the cursor keys. When you have pressed Enter twice, you will be asked whether you wish to export the entire worksheet or only a certain range:

```
                Lotus  1-2-3  Release 2.4 Translate Utility
   Copr. 1985, 1991, 1992  Lotus Development Corporation  All Rights Reserved

   Translate FROM: 1-2-3 2.4              Translate TO: dBase III

   Source file: C:\123R24\SECCAR2.WK1

   Target file: C:\123R24\SECCAR2.DBF


       ┌─────────────────────────────────┐
       │  Translate entire worksheet     │
       │  Worksheet  Range               │
       └─────────────────────────────────┘
```

Having chosen the required option, confirm it using Enter. Then the question whether you want to proceed with the translation will appear. By answering Yes, you will set the procedure in motion. When the file has been translated satisfactorily the program will state the message 'Translation successful.

However, there are preconditions linked to the translation of a file from 1-2-3 to dBase:

- The entire file or range must be a database.
- The first row of the file or range must consist of field names.
- The second row must contain the first record.
- Columns must be wide enough to display the data, otherwise data will be cut off during conversion.
- Between 1 and 128 data fields are possible.

5.2.2   Importing files from other programs

If files from other programs must be adopted, you may choose from various versions of Lotus, dBase, EN-ABLE, DIF, Multiplan, SuperCalc, Symphony (various versions) and VisiCalc files. This can be useful, for instance, if other spreadsheets are also used within a company. Files from these programs can also be edited. Another possibility is the processing of a database from dBase using Lotus 1-2-3. The data from the database are converted to a 1-2-3 worksheet file (.WK1) and may subsequently be processed in the usual way.

Below, we shall use a Multiplan file called ORDER as an example to be imported. To do this, the Multiplan file must first be saved in the SYLK format. Specify the extension .SLK.

Activate the Translate utility program. Then choose the source program, in this case, Multiplan. Go to it using the cursor keys and press Enter. This should produce the following screen:

```
                    Lotus  1-2-3  Release 2.4 Translate Utility
        Copr. 1985, 1991, 1992  Lotus Development Corporation  All Rights Reserved


        Translate FROM: Multiplan (SYLK)    What do you want to translate TO?

                                            1-2-3 1A
                                            1-2-3 2 through 2.4
                                            Symphony 1.0
                                            Symphony 1.1 through 2.2








                    Move the menu pointer to your selection and press ENTER
                        Press ESC to return to the source product menu
                            Press F1 (HELP) for more information
```

Specify here the target program. Some remarks concerning this particular conversion will be shown. Quit this information screen using Esc and you can specify the required source file from the list displayed. You can change directory using Esc, if required. Then press Enter twice and affirm the question whether the conversion should take place. You will observe on the screen that the program translates the file. Messages will be given concerning the efficiency of the conversion.

The procedure is thus as follows:

■ Activate the Translate utility program using 'trans' at the DOS command line or the Translate option from the Access menu.
■ Go to the required source program using the cursor keys and confirm this choice using Enter.
■ Go to the required target program using the cursor keys and confirm the choice using Enter.
■ In the same way, select a file to be converted. Change directory, if necessary, using the Esc key.
■ Implement the conversion by specifying Yes and pressing Enter.

The result of the conversion can be shown by activating it in the normal way in 1-2-3, thus using File Retrieve.

5.3   1-2-3 and its companion programs

Version 2.4 of Lotus 1-2-3 includes several companion programs which extend the features of 1-2-3. To use 1-2-3 and its companion programs, you require at least 5 Mb of free disk space.

Checking your harddisk space

If you are not sure whether you have enough space on your harddisk for version 2.4 of Lotus 1-2-3 and its companion programs, follow the instructions below:

1. At the operating system prompt, make the harddisk drive which will contain your program files the current drive. For example, if you plan to use 1-2-3 on drive C, type c: and press Enter.

2. Type dir and press Enter.

    At the bottom of the list of files, the operating system displays the amount of bytes free, which is the amount of available space on the harddisk. If you do not have at least 5 Mb available, you may want to delete unwanted files from your harddisk or transfer fewer companion programs. The install program provides instructions for transferring all the programs or only the programs you want.

The following table lists 1-2-3 and its companion programs:

program name	description
SmartIcons	Lets you perform 1-2-3 tasks by selecting icons on the screen.
Wysiwyg	Lets you format, print and add graphics to the worksheets you create. Includes SmartPics files (.CGM files).

Add-Ins

Auditor, Backsolver, Viewer and Macro Library Manager add features to 1-2-3.

1-2-3-Go!

Online tutorial which teaches you how to use 1-2-3 during a 1-2-3 session.

Wysiwyg-Go!

Online tutorial which shows you how to use the Wysiwyg add-in to create more professional-looking worksheets.

PrintGraph

Lets you display and print the graphs you created in 1-2-3. (Unless you plan to use a pen plotter or print several graphs at the same time, you do not need to transfer PrintGraph.)

Translate

Lets you use data from other spreadsheet and database management programs in 1-2-3 or lets you convert worksheets so that other programs can read them. (Unless you plan to convert worksheets from other programs, you do not need to transfer the Translate utility.)

Unless you specify a different combination of companion programs, the Install program automatically transfers 1-2-3 and SmartIcons, Wysiwyg and SmartPics files (.CGM), Add-ins, 1-2-3-Go! and Wysiwyg-Go! to your harddisk. The Install program does not transfer PrintGraph and Translate unless you select them.

The Install program sets up 1-2-3 so that it activates SmartIcons (and Wysiwyg if you installed it) automatically every time you start a work session. In addition, **SmartIcons** is assigned to **Alt-F7**.

5.3.1   SmartIcons

The SmartIcons add-in is a new program which displays **icons** (either graphic images or, if Wysiwyg is not attached, text representations of the images) which you can select to perform a 1-2-3 or Wysiwyg task. If you attached SmartIcons, you can now use an icon by selecting the icon using the mouse or by pressing the Alt-key combination you assigned to SmartIcons, selecting the icon using the arrow keys and pressing Enter. For example, when you highlight a range and select the icon which represents /Range Format Percent, 1-2-3 formats all the cells in that range as percentages.

When you activate an icon, a brief description of its function appears in the control panel.

The SmartIcon add-in provides a total of 77 icons organized in palettes. A **palette** is a column of icons which appears at the right of the worksheet. The total number of palettes you have depends on your screen display (CGA, EGA or VGA) and on whether or not Wysiwyg is attached.

The first palette is the custom palette because you can modify it to display the icons you use most frequently. The custom palette is identified by the <-1-> which appears at the bottom of the column of icons.

The icons on the remaining palettes are fixed. The last palette contains the icons U1 to U12. These are the **user icons** to which you can assign macros.

Selecting an icon using the mouse:

1. If the icon you wish to use is not on the current palette, click on the arrow on either side of the palette number to scroll backwards or forwards to the correct palette.
2. Click on the icon you wish to use.

Selecting an icon using the keyboard:

1. Press Alt-7 or the key you assigned to SmartIcons when you attached it. 1-2-3 highlights the first icon in the current palette.
2. Move the highlight to the icon you want.

Press	To
Cursor left	Move the highlight to the previous icon palette.
Cursor right	Move the highlight to the next icon palette.
Cursor up	Move the highlight to the previous icon.
Cursor down	Move the highlight to the next icon.
END	Move the highlight to the last icon in the current palette.
HOME	Move the highlight to the first icon on the current palette.

3. Press Enter to select the icon you want.

To add an icon to your custom palette

1. Select Add Icon.
   1-2-3 highlights the first icon on the current palette and displays a message which explains how to select an icon for a custom palette.
2. Select the icon you want to add to your custom palette.
   1-2-3 inserts a copy of the icon at the bottom of the custom palette and displays the custom palette on the screen. If the custom palette was full before you added the new icon to it, 1-2-3 removes the bottom icon to make room for the new icon.

To remove an icon from your custom palette

1. Select Del Icon.
   1-2-3 displays your custom palette.

2. Select the icon you wish to remove from the custom palette.
    1-2-3 removes the icon from the custom palette.

To move an icon on your custom palette

1. Select Move Icon.
    1-2-3 displays your custom palette.
2. Select the icon you wish to move.
    1-2-3 replaces the icon with a blank icon.
3. Select the icon at the location where you want the icon you are moving to appear.
    The icon you selected in step 2 appears at the new location, and 1-2-3 repositions the other icons to make room for the icon you moved.

To assign a macro to a user icon

1. Move to the penultimate palette and select User Icon.
    The User Icon Descriptions dialogue box appears.
2. Select the user icon to which you want to assign a macro.
3. Select Assign Macro to Icon.
    The User-Defined Icon dialogue box appears.
4. In the Icon Description text box, type a description of the macro using a maximum of 72 characters.
    1-2-3 uses this text for the description which appears in the control panel when you highlight the icon and for the description which appears in the User Icon Descriptions dialogue box.
5. In the Macro Text box, type the macro instructions using a maximum of 240 characters.
    A macro may include the following:
    keystroke sequences which represent 1-2-3, Wysiwyg and add-in commands; the {BRANCH} command; macro keywords which correspond to the standard keyboard keys and the 1-2-3 function keys, for example, {DOWN}.

You can run a macro assigned to a user icon by selecting the user icon, just as you would select any other icon. For instance, if you assign a macro which enters your company name in a cell to user icon U2 and then select U2, 1-2-3 enters the company name in the current cell.

5.3.2 Add-ins

Lotus 1-2-3 provides a broad spectrum of functions. Nevertheless, there are still more users who require more extended functions in practice. For this group of users, many extra programs have become available in the meantime, the so-called *add-ins*, which are supplied by both the Lotus Corporation and others.

Attaching Add-ins

If you cancelled automatic start-up of SmartIcons and/or Wysiwyg, but you wish to use one of these Add-ins or any other 1-2-3 add-in in the current work session, you must first attach the add-in you wish to use. When you attach an add-in, it stays in memory during the 1-2-3 work session or until you select /Add-in Detach.

1. Select /Add-in Attach.
2. Select one of the following:
    AUDITOR.ADN   Specifies the Auditor add-in
    BSOLVER.ADN   Specifies the Backsolver add-in
    ICONS.ADN   Specifies the SmartIcons add-in
    MACROMGR.ADN   Specifies the Macro Library Manager add-in
    TUTOR.ADN   Specifies the 1-2-3-Go! add-in
    VIEWER.ADN   Specifies the Viewer add-in
    WYSIWYG.ADN   Specifies the Wysiwyg add-in

3. When 1-2-3 asks you to select a key, select one of the following: 7, 8, 9 or 10.
    Select a number if you want to use the keyboard to

activate the add-in. The number you select specifies
the key you want to use to activate the add-in. For
example. if you select 8, Alt-F8 becomes the key
which activates the add-in.
Select No-Key if you are attaching Wysiwyg.

4. Select Quit to return to the READY mode.

If you attached Wysiwyg, you can now display the
commands on the Wysiwyg menu by pressing the
colon (:) or by moving the mouse pointer to the control panel and clicking the right mouse button.

Backsolver Add-In

The Backsolver add-in is a new add-in program which
allows you to calculate a formula to achieve a given
value by changing one or more of the variables which
affect the result of the formula. For instance, you may
have a specific profit margin target to achieve and you
need to know the total sales required in order to reach
that target. You tell Backsolver the extent of the profit
margin and then specify the cell whose value you want
to alter to reach that profit margin (the total sales cell).
Backsolver will calculate the value the total sales need
to reach in order to equal the target.

To use Backsolver

1. Enter the formula to be solved by Backsolver in a
    cell.
2. Decide the desired result of the formula and which
    variable to change.
3. Attach and invoke Backsolver.
4. Select Formula-Cell and specify the address of the
    cell which contains the formula you want Backsolver
    to solve.
5. Select Value and specify the value you want the for-
    mula in the formula cell to be when the problem is
    solved.
    You can enter either a number or a formula. If you

enter a formula, Backsolver reduces the formula to a
value before calculating the problem.
6. Select Adjustable and specify the adjustable cell(s),
    in other words, the cells which contain the values
    which Backsolver can change.
    The formula cell must refer to the adjustable cell(s)
    either directly or indirectly. You can specify a single
    cell or a range of cells.
7. Select Solve.
    1-2-3 changes the value or values in the adjustable
    cells so that the formula produces the value you
    specified and returns 1-2-3 to the READY mode. If
    other formulas depend on the solved formula or on
    the adjustable cells, 1-2-3 recalculates these cells
    also.

Caution: When you use Backsolver to solve a problem,
1-2-3 replaces the original values in the adjustable cells
with the values Backsolver calculates.

SmartPics

SmartPics are ready made graphic objects which you
can place in a worksheet. SmartPics give worksheets a
professional touch, add visual interest and reinforce the
message. SmartPics are stored in files which have the
extension .CGM. If you choose to transfer Wysiwyg files
to your harddisk during installation, Install automatically
transfers SmartPics to your 1-2-3 program directory. To
use SmartPics, select :(colon) Graph Add Metafile,
specify the .CGM file you want to include in the worksheet, and specify the range in which you want the
graphic object to appear. You can then use :Graph Edit
to resize or enhance the graphic object.

Another add-in which is provided as standard from version 2.2 onwards is the **Macro Library Manager.** With
this utility program, it is possible to save well-used macros, formulas and data tables separately, so that you
can use them in various worksheets without having to
repeatedly specify all commands and data time and
again.

This program is also activated using the Add-in command from the main menu where you will find the file name MACROMGR.ADN. Go to it using the highlight bar and press Enter. Ranges in the worksheet containing macros can now be saved in the macro library using the Save command. The extension .MLB is automatically added.

Users who require a more professional printout of their work, were able to make use of the **Always** utility program from Funk software in previous Lotus versions. Lotus 1-2-3 provides this add-in program as standard in versions 2.2 and 2.3, although it is no longer supplied with the most recent version. Nevertheless, it can be purchased separately and still functions excellently as an Add-in. When the worksheet has been made in the normal way in 1-2-3, you are able to load the Allways program using the Add-in instruction from the main menu. Subsequently, you have the possibility of assigning a certain key to the program which allows you to activate the program directly from the worksheet. For instance, if you assign F8 to the Allways program, you can activate the program directly from the current worksheet using the Alt-F8 key combination.

Whether you assign a key to Allways or not, you can activate the program using the Start command from the menu which subsequently appears. Just as with 1-2-3, you can activate the main menu by pressing the backslash.

Allways provides various possibilities of presenting charts and tables in a more representative way. Among other things, this program:

■ provides a zoom function to enlarge or reduce the display on the screen
■ can insert charts in the worksheet
■ offers a large choice of different fonts
■ provides the possibility of adding borders, shading and underlining to certain ranges
■ creating sheets for overhead projection.

Printing in landscape mode

Version 2.4 of Lotus 1-2-3 allows you to print to a dot-matrix or laser printer using **landscape mode** (along the length of the paper). You specify the mode you want by using the Wysiwyg command :(colon) Print Config Orientation.

In addition to these programs, there are a number of other utility programs for Lotus 1-2-3 on the market. These programs are also loaded using the Add-in instruction. If you place them in the current directory, they will be automatically shown in the Add-in list of files. Otherwise, you will have to specify the appropriate drive and directory.

One of these products is the Impress program from Aleph 2 which also deals with an improved presentation of charts and tables. It covers the same application area as Allways. The improvements concern both display on the screen and printout from the printer.

Special details:

■ You can make use of the possibilities of colour monitors by defining different colours for the background, unprotected cells, cell pointer and borders.
■ You may choose from various fonts and letter sizes.
■ You can add stripes, borders, charts and table layouts.

The use of the Sideways program can also be interesting. Using this, it is possible to turn spreadsheets 90 degrees when printing. This can be important when working with broad worksheets.

In order to integrate worksheets in reports and other texts, the add-in program Inword from Funk software can be very useful. In addition to the normal functions, this program provides:

■ extensive edit functions

■ layout features such as page numeration, centring and tabs
■ print function such as various fonts and proportional letters
■ complete macro compatibility with Lotus 1-2-3.

The Silverado program from Computer Associates is provided as an add-in database for Lotus 1-2-3. Using this program, Lotus 1-2-3 can be extended to a complete relational database. It is a program which is managed using menus, supporting all 1-2-3 possibilities. Special details are:

■ display of data in the form of masks or tables
■ relationships between fields of one record or between fields of records adjacent to one another
■ combines own functions with @ functions
■ interim balance after replacement of a group or total balance.

Index